THE DREAM DICTIONARY FOR BEGINNERS

THE DREAM DICTIONARY FOR BEGINNERS

A PRACTICAL GUIDE TO UNDERSTANDING YOUR DREAMS

Isobel Chaucer

www.blkdogpublishing.com

Unlock the mysteries of your subconscious with *The Dream Dictionary for Beginners: A Practical Guide to Understanding Your Dreams.*

This comprehensive guide offers clear, insightful interpretations of both common and unusual dream symbols, helping you uncover the messages your mind is sending while you sleep. Whether you're dreaming of flying, falling, or something more obscure, this book will guide you in understanding the deeper meanings behind your nightly visions.

Designed for dreamers of all levels, this book combines psychological and spiritual insights to provide a well-rounded approach to dream interpretation. With easy-to-navigate A-Z chapters, practical tips for enhancing dream recall, and thoughtful advice on how to use your dreams for personal growth, this friendly guide is your perfect companion for exploring the fascinating world of dreams.

"The dream is a little hidden door in the innermost recesses of the psyche."
— **Carl Jung**

Before You Begin: A Note from the Author

"Dreams are the royal road to the unconscious." — **Sigmund Freud**

I know you're probably eager to dive straight into the dream meanings, but before you do, I encourage you to read the initial chapters of this book first. These chapters provide essential guidance on how to enhance your dream recall, interpret symbols, and understand the deeper messages within your dreams. By taking the time to explore these fundamental ideas, you'll be better equipped to unlock the full potential of your dreams and gain profound insights into your inner world.

Happy dreaming!

Isobel Chaucer

INTRODUCTION

"You are never too old to set another goal or to dream a new dream."
– C.S. Lewis

Dreams have fascinated humans for centuries. They are mysterious, elusive, and often surreal experiences that occur while we sleep. For some, dreams are mere fragments of thoughts or events experienced during the day, while for others they are profound journeys filled with symbols, messages, and hidden meanings. The study of dreams, or oneirology, seeks to understand these nightly narratives and unlock the secrets they hold.

Dreams can be a reflection of our innermost thoughts, desires, fears, and unresolved issues. They can be a window into our subconscious mind, revealing what we might not fully understand about ourselves in our waking life. Some believe dreams can predict the future, provide guidance, or serve as a creative muse. Whether you see dreams as random brain activity or as a meaningful phenomenon, understanding their symbolism can offer valuable insights into your psyche.

This book is designed to help you explore the world of dreams. Organised in an A-Z format, it provides interpretations for a wide range of common and obscure dream symbols. From flying and falling to encountering animals or strange beings, each entry aims to guide you through the labyrinth of meanings and associations tied to these nocturnal visions. As you read through, you'll gain a deeper understanding of how to interpret your own dreams and apply these interpretations to your life

THE POWER OF DAILY JOURNALING: ENHANCING DREAM JOURNALING AND RECOGNISING THEMES

"Dreams are the touchstones of our characters."
– Henry David Thoreau

Journaling is a powerful tool that extends far beyond simply writing down daily events or dreams. It is a practice that can enhance self-awareness, provide emotional clarity, and foster personal growth. When it comes to understanding your dreams, journaling your daily experiences and emotions can play a crucial role. This chapter explores the benefits of daily journaling, how it complements dream journaling, and how it can help you identify recurring themes and patterns in both your waking and dreaming life.

THE CONNECTION BETWEEN DAILY JOURNALING AND DREAM JOURNALING

Dreams are deeply connected to our waking life—they reflect our thoughts, emotions, experiences, and even our unresolved conflicts. By keeping a daily journal alongside a dream journal, you create a comprehensive record of your inner and outer worlds. This practice allows for a more profound understanding of how your daily life influences your dreams and vice versa.

INCREASED AWARENESS OF EMOTIONS AND EXPERIENCES:

Daily journaling encourages you to become more aware of your emotions and experiences. By writing about your day, you are more likely to notice the thoughts, feelings, and events that have impacted you most. This heightened awareness can carry over into your dream journaling, helping you to recall dreams more vividly and to identify emotional undercurrents that may have surfaced during sleep.

RECOGNISING TRIGGERS AND PATTERNS:

Keeping a journal of your daily life allows you to recognise triggers and patterns that may influence your dreams. For example, if you notice that stressful days at work often lead to dreams of being chased or feeling trapped, you can begin to connect these dots and explore how your daily stressors are manifesting in your dreams. By identifying these patterns, you can gain insights into your subconscious mind and work on addressing any underlying issues.

Bridging the Gap Between Waking and Dreaming Life:

Our waking life and dreams are not separate—they are interconnected realms that influence one another. By journaling both your daily experiences and your dreams, you bridge the gap between these two worlds. This practice allows you to see how your daily life may influence your dreams and how your dreams might be reflecting or responding to your waking experiences. Understanding this connection can lead to greater self-awareness and personal growth.

Enhancing Memory and Dream Recall:

Regular journaling, both of daily experiences and dreams, can improve memory and dream recall. When you write down your experiences, you engage your memory and cognitive processes, making it easier to remember details. This practice can translate into better dream recall, as the habit of journaling trains your mind to remember and record experiences, whether waking or dreaming. Over time, you may find that you can remember your dreams more clearly and in greater detail.

How to Journal Your Day to Enhance Dream Journaling"

To maximise the benefits of journaling for dream interpretation, it's essential to establish a consistent practice that captures both your daily experiences and your dreams. Here are some tips on how to effectively journal your day to enhance your dream journaling:

SET ASIDE TIME FOR JOURNALING:

Dedicate a specific time each day for journaling, preferably in the evening before bed. This practice allows you to reflect on the day's events, emotions, and experiences, creating a mental bridge to the dream state. Regular journaling helps reinforce the habit, making it more likely that you will remember and record your dreams upon waking.

CAPTURE KEY EVENTS AND EMOTIONS:

When journaling your day, focus on key events, interactions, and emotions that stood out to you. Pay attention to moments of high emotional intensity, whether positive or negative, as these are often the experiences most likely to influence your dreams. Note any unresolved feelings or conflicts, as these may surface in your dreams as your subconscious mind works through them.

EXPLORE THOUGHTS AND REFLECTIONS:

Beyond just recording events, use your journal to explore your thoughts and reflections about the day. Consider how certain experiences made you feel, what thoughts they triggered, and any insights or lessons you gained. Reflecting on your day in this way can help you understand how your conscious mind is processing your experiences, which in turn can provide clues about your dreams.

IDENTIFY RECURRING THEMES AND PATTERNS:

As you continue to journal daily, start looking for recurring themes or patterns in both your waking and dreaming life. Are there certain emotions, experiences, or symbols that keep appearing? For example, you might notice a recurring theme of feeling unprepared or out of control, both in daily situations and in your dreams. Identifying these patterns can help you understand what your subconscious mind is trying to communicate and what areas of your life may need attention or healing.

COMPARE WAKING AND DREAM SYMBOLS:

Use your daily journal to compare symbols and themes that appear in both your waking and dreaming life. For instance, if you frequently encounter water in your dreams and have noted a recent increase in waking experiences involving water (e.g., spending time near a lake, having conversations about the ocean), this could suggest a significant symbolic connection. Exploring these connections can provide deeper insights into the messages your dreams are conveying.

WRITE FREELY AND WITHOUT JUDGMENT:

When journaling, write freely and without self-censorship. Allow your thoughts and emotions to flow naturally onto the page. This practice helps you connect more deeply with your subconscious mind and can reveal insights that might not emerge through more structured or controlled writing. Embracing a non-judgmental approach encourages honesty and self-exploration, both crucial for understanding your dreams.

RECOGNISING THEMES AND PATTERNS ACROSS TIME

As you continue the practice of daily and dream journaling, you may begin to notice broader themes and patterns that emerge over time. These might include recurring dreams, symbols, or emotional themes that reflect ongoing life challenges, growth, or transformation.

TRACKING EMOTIONAL STATES:

Regular journaling can help you track your emotional states over time and how they correlate with your dreams. You might notice that periods of high stress or anxiety in your waking life lead to more vivid or intense dreams, or that feelings of joy and contentment are reflected in more peaceful, positive dreams.

UNDERSTANDING LIFE TRANSITIONS:

Journaling can provide a valuable record of how your dreams

change during significant life transitions, such as moving to a new place, starting a new job, or ending a relationship. By reviewing your journals, you can gain insights into how these transitions are affecting you on both a conscious and subconscious levels.

SPOTTING GROWTH AND HEALING:

Over time, journaling can help you recognise signs of personal growth and healing. You may notice a shift in your dreams from themes of fear or conflict to themes of empowerment or resolution, reflecting your inner healing process. This awareness can encourage further self-reflection and personal development.

CREATING A DIALOGUE BETWEEN YOUR WAKING AND DREAMING SELVES:

By journaling your daily life and dreams, you create a continuous dialogue between your waking and dreaming selves. This dialogue helps you understand how your conscious mind is processing your subconscious experiences and vice versa, leading to greater self-awareness and integration of your inner and outer worlds.

CONCLUSION:

Daily journaling is a powerful practice that complements dream journaling, offering a holistic approach to understanding the interconnectedness of our waking and dreaming lives. By recording and reflecting on both daily experiences and dreams, you can gain deeper insights into your subconscious mind, identify recurring themes and patterns, and foster personal growth and healing. Embracing the practice of journaling as a daily ritual allows you to better understand yourself, your dreams, and the intricate dance between your conscious and subconscious worlds.

How to Record Your Dreams

"I think that our dreams are a manifestation of our subconscious mind. I think they're often a reflection of what's going on in our lives."
— Jennifer Aniston

Interpreting dreams begins with recalling them. As dreams can often fade quickly upon waking, keeping a dream journal is an essential practice. Here are some tips to help you accurately capture the details of your dreams:

Keep a Journal by Your Bedside:

Place a notebook and pen, or a digital recorder, within easy reach of your bed. This way, as soon as you wake up, you can jot down your dreams before they begin to fade.

Record Immediately Upon Waking:

As soon as you wake up, try to remain still and keep your eyes closed for a moment. This will help you stay connected to the dream world and retain the details. Start writing as soon as possible, capturing everything you remember, no matter how trivial it may seem.

WRITE IN DETAIL:

Describe the environment, people, emotions, colours, sounds, and any other sensations you experienced in the dream. Pay attention to specific symbols, objects, or actions that stood out to you. Even seemingly insignificant details could hold meaning.

REFLECT ON YOUR EMOTIONS:

How did you feel during the dream? Your emotional response can be a key indicator of what the dream is trying to convey. Note any shifts in emotions, as they can provide additional context to the dream's meaning.

CONSIDER PATTERNS AND THEMES:

Over time, as you continue to record your dreams, you may notice recurring themes, symbols, or scenarios. These patterns can offer deeper insights into your subconscious mind and the issues you may be grappling with in your waking life.

REVIEW YOUR ENTRIES REGULARLY:

Make it a habit to review your dream journal entries regularly. Look for connections between your dreams and your waking experiences. You may discover that your dreams reflect unresolved emotions, ongoing challenges, or unacknowledged desires.

ENHANCING DREAM RECALL AND TECHNIQUES FOR LUCID DREAMING

"In dreams, we enter a world that is entirely our own."
— Steven Spielberg

Dreams are a powerful tool for self-discovery and introspection. However, for many people, remembering dreams can be a challenge. In this chapter, we will explore techniques to improve dream recall and introduce the concept of lucid dreaming—a state in which the dreamer becomes aware that they are dreaming and can sometimes influence the dream's direction. Both practices can significantly enrich your dream life and deepen your understanding of your subconscious mind.

SET AN INTENTION BEFORE SLEEP:

Before going to bed, set a clear intention to remember your dreams. This can be as simple as saying, "Tonight, I will remember my dreams." Repeating this affirmation helps prime your mind to retain dream memories upon waking.

Maintain a Regular Sleep Schedule:

Consistent sleep patterns improve the quality of your sleep, which can lead to more vivid dreams and better recall. Aim for 7-9 hours of sleep each night and try to go to bed and wake up at the same time every day.

Reduce Stimulants Before Bed:

Avoid consuming caffeine, alcohol, or heavy meals at least a few hours before sleep. These substances can interfere with the REM (Rapid Eye Movement) stage of sleep, where most vivid dreaming occurs.

Wake Up Slowly:

Upon waking, try to stay still and keep your eyes closed. This helps you remain in a semi-dream state, allowing you to recall the details more easily. Gently bring your attention to any dream fragments or feelings, and then begin writing them down.

Use a Dream Journal:

As mentioned earlier, keeping a dream journal by your bedside is crucial. Write down your dreams immediately upon waking, capturing as much detail as possible. Over time, this practice can significantly improve your dream recall and help you identify patterns.

MINDFULNESS AND MEDITATION:

Practising mindfulness and meditation can enhance your awareness in both waking and dream states. Meditation before bed helps calm the mind, making it easier to remember dreams. Additionally, mindfulness exercises throughout the day can increase your awareness in dreams, leading to more vivid experiences.

EXPERIMENT WITH SLEEP CYCLES:

Dreams are most vivid during the REM phase of sleep, which becomes longer and more frequent in the latter part of the sleep cycle. Experimenting with sleep duration or setting an alarm for about 90 minutes after falling asleep (the average length of a sleep cycle) can help wake you up during REM sleep, increasing the likelihood of recalling your dreams.

TECHNIQUES FOR LUCID DREAMING:

Lucid dreaming occurs when you become aware that you are dreaming while still in the dream. This awareness can sometimes allow you to control or influence the dream. Lucid dreaming can be a thrilling experience, offering opportunities for self-exploration, creativity, and overcoming fears. Here are some techniques to help you achieve lucid dreams:

REALITY CHECKS:

Throughout the day, perform "reality checks" to determine whether you are dreaming. This could be as simple as looking at your hands and asking, "Am I dreaming?" or checking the time twice in quick succession (time often appears distorted in dreams). With regular practice, these checks can become a habit that carries over into your dreams, helping you realise you're dreaming.

WAKE-BACK-TO-BED (WBTB) METHOD:

This technique involves waking up after 4-6 hours of sleep, staying awake for 20-30 minutes (during which you focus on your intention to lucid dream), and then returning to sleep. The idea is to enter REM sleep directly upon returning to bed, increasing the chances of lucid dreaming.

MNEMONIC INDUCTION OF LUCID DREAMS (MILD):

Before falling asleep, repeat a phrase like "The next time I'm dreaming, I will realise I'm dreaming." Visualise yourself becoming aware in a dream. This technique relies on prospective memory, or the intention to remember to do something in the future, to increase the likelihood of lucidity.

Keep a Lucid Dream Journal:

In addition to your regular dream journal, keep a separate section for lucid dreams. Write down any successful attempts, noting what triggered your awareness and any techniques that worked. Reflecting on these entries can reinforce your ability to recognise dream signs.

Visualisation and Affirmations:

Before sleep, spend a few minutes visualising yourself becoming lucid in a dream. Imagine the sensation of realising you're dreaming and what you would do next. Combine this with affirmations like "I am aware of my dreams" to set a clear intention.

Mindfulness and Dream Awareness:

Develop a habit of observing your surroundings with heightened awareness throughout the day. Pay attention to details, question your reality, and cultivate a sense of curiosity. This heightened state of awareness can transfer to your dreams, increasing the likelihood of becoming lucid.

SUPPLEMENTATION:

Certain natural supplements, like vitamin B6, galantamine, or mugwort, are believed to enhance dream vividness and lucidity. However, it's essential to consult a healthcare professional before trying any supplements to ensure they are safe and appropriate for you.

By practising these techniques, you can improve your dream recall and increase your chances of experiencing lucid dreams. Both practices can provide a deeper understanding of your subconscious mind, allowing you to explore the limitless world of dreams with greater clarity and purpose.

Isobel Chaucer

CHAPTER: NIGHTMARES: EXPLORING THE DARK SIDE OF DREAMS

"Dreams are illustrations from the book your soul is writing about you."
— *Marsha Norman*

Dreams can often transport us to realms of wonder and insight, but they can also lead us into darker, more unsettling territory. Nightmares—those vivid, distressing dreams that evoke strong negative emotions such as fear, anxiety, or sadness—are a universal human experience. While nightmares can be unsettling, they offer a unique opportunity for self-discovery and healing when approached with a holistic mindset. In this chapter, we will explore nightmares from a holistic perspective, examining their causes, potential meanings, and methods for understanding and integrating these challenging experiences.

UNDERSTANDING NIGHTMARES: A HOLISTIC PERSPECTIVE:

Nightmares are more than just frightening experiences during sleep; they are profound psychological events that can reflect our deepest fears, unresolved conflicts, and even our physical well-being. A holistic approach to understanding nightmares involves recognising them as part of the broader tapestry of our emotional, mental, and spiritual lives. This perspective invites us to view nightmares not merely as disturbances to be eliminated but as messages from the subconscious that can provide valuable insights.

From a holistic viewpoint, nightmares are seen as an expression of the subconscious mind, seeking to communicate with the conscious self. They can serve as a form of emotional release, allowing us to process unresolved feelings or confront aspects of our inner world that need attention. Rather than fearing these dreams, we can approach them with curiosity and openness, seeking to understand the messages they carry.

COMMON CAUSES OF NIGHTMARES: AN INTEGRATED VIEW:

Nightmares can be triggered by a variety of factors, including psychological stress, trauma, physical health, lifestyle choices, and spiritual imbalances. Understanding these triggers from a holistic standpoint involves considering how these factors interact and influence our dreams.

EMOTIONAL STRESS AND ANXIETY:

Emotional stress and anxiety are some of the most common causes of nightmares. When we are under emotional strain, our minds may use dreams as a way to process and release pent-up emotions. From a holistic perspective, nightmares resulting from stress or anxiety are seen as the subconscious mind's attempt to bring awareness to unresolved issues or emotional pain, inviting us to address these challenges in waking life.

TRAUMA AND UNPROCESSED EMOTIONS:

Trauma, both recent and from the past, can significantly impact dream content. Nightmares related to trauma may involve reliving distressing events or encountering symbolic representations of the trauma. A holistic approach encourages viewing these nightmares as opportunities for healing, suggesting that the mind is attempting to process and integrate traumatic experiences. Working with a therapist or engaging in practices such as journaling, meditation, or creative expression can help facilitate this process.

PHYSICAL HEALTH AND WELL-BEING:

Nightmares can also be linked to physical health issues, such as illness, pain, or medication side effects. For example, a fever can cause vivid, disturbing dreams, while certain medications may alter brain chemistry in ways that affect dream content. From a holistic perspective, these nightmares may be seen as the body's way of communicating its needs. Paying attention to these dreams can offer insights into our physical well-being, prompting us to take better care of our health through proper nutrition, exercise, and regular medical check-ups.

Spiritual Imbalances:

In some holistic traditions, nightmares are thought to reflect spiritual imbalances or unresolved spiritual issues. These might include feelings of disconnection, existential fears, or struggles with one's sense of purpose or identity. Nightmares of this nature may serve as a call to engage more deeply with one's spiritual practice, whether through meditation, prayer, mindfulness, or other forms of spiritual exploration. Recognising the spiritual dimensions of nightmares can help us understand them as part of a broader journey toward self-realisation and wholeness.

Lifestyle Factors and Environmental Influences:

Holistic approaches also consider how lifestyle choices, such as diet, exercise, and sleep hygiene, affect dream content. Consuming stimulating substances like caffeine or alcohol, eating heavy meals before bed, or engaging in stressful activities late at night can contribute to nightmares. Creating a calming evening routine, practising relaxation techniques, and ensuring a peaceful sleep environment can help reduce the likelihood of distressing dreams.

Interpreting Nightmares: A Path to Self-Discovery:

Nightmares, while frightening, can be rich in symbolism and meaning. Interpreting these dreams through a holistic lens involves understanding them as part of our personal narrative, reflecting our inner world and the challenges we face.

COPING WITH NIGHTMARES: HOLISTIC STRATEGIES:

While nightmares can be challenging, several holistic strategies can help reduce their frequency and intensity and transform them into opportunities for growth and healing.

MINDFULNESS AND MEDITATION:

Practising mindfulness and meditation can help calm the mind and reduce the anxiety that often contributes to nightmares. Mindfulness encourages a non-judgmental awareness of the present moment, helping us to let go of fear and anxiety. Meditation can help create a sense of inner peace and balance, making it easier to cope with distressing dreams.

DREAM JOURNALING AND REFLECTION:

Keeping a dream journal can be a powerful tool for understanding nightmares. By writing down dreams as soon as we wake, we can begin to identify patterns and themes. Reflecting on these dreams with curiosity and openness allows us to uncover hidden messages and insights, providing opportunities for self-exploration and healing. Journaling can also help us externalise and process our fears, reducing their emotional impact.

Creative Expression:

Engaging in creative activities, such as drawing, painting, or writing, can help us explore and process the emotions and themes present in our nightmares. By giving form to our fears and anxieties, we can gain a deeper understanding of their origins and meaning. Creative expression can also provide a sense of empowerment, transforming nightmares into a source of inspiration and growth.

Guided Imagery and Visualisation:

Guided imagery and visualisation techniques can help transform nightmares by encouraging us to reimagine their content in a more positive or empowering light. By visualising a different outcome or introducing protective elements into the dream scenario, we can reduce the emotional intensity of nightmares and foster a sense of control over our inner world.

Seeking Support:

Sometimes, nightmares can be too overwhelming to handle alone. Seeking support from a therapist, counsellor, or support group can provide a safe space to explore and understand the emotions and experiences underlying nightmares. Professional guidance can help identify patterns, address unresolved trauma, and develop coping strategies that support holistic healing.

Transforming Nightmares: Embracing the Shadow:

From a holistic standpoint, nightmares are an invitation to engage with the darker aspects of our psyche—those parts of ourselves that we may fear, reject, or misunderstand. By approaching nightmares with curiosity and compassion, we can transform them from terrifying experiences into valuable opportunities for self-discovery and healing.

Shadow Work and Self-Integration:

Shadow work involves exploring and integrating the hidden or repressed parts of ourselves, often symbolised by the content of nightmares. By facing these aspects with an open heart and mind, we can begin to heal old wounds, release unprocessed emotions, and embrace a more authentic self.

Embracing Nightmares as Teachers:

Viewing nightmares as teachers, rather than threats, can help shift our relationship with them. Instead of avoiding or fearing nightmares, we can welcome them as opportunities for growth, inviting us to confront and understand our deepest fears and desires. This shift in perspective can reduce the power nightmares have over us and empower us to take an active role in our healing journey.

Cultivating a Sense of Safety and Protection:

Creating a sense of safety and protection in both waking and dreaming life can help reduce the impact of nightmares. This might involve developing a bedtime ritual that includes calming practices such as lighting a candle, playing soothing music, or using aromatherapy. Surrounding oneself with comforting symbols or objects can also help create a sense of security and reduce fear.

The Gift of Nightmares:

While nightmares can be unsettling and even frightening, they offer a unique opportunity to explore the depths of our subconscious and address unresolved issues. By approaching nightmares with a holistic mindset, we can transform them from sources of fear into powerful tools for self-awareness, healing, and growth.

A-Z Dream Dictionary

This book will provide an extensive A-Z dream dictionary, covering a wide range of symbols and scenarios. Each entry will include a detailed explanation of the possible meanings behind the dream symbol, considering both psychological interpretations and cultural or historical contexts.

By exploring these entries and considering the context of your own dreams, you will be able to gain deeper insights into your subconscious mind and unlock the mysteries that lie within.

Isobel Chaucer

A

Abandonment

Dreaming of abandonment often signifies feelings of insecurity or fear of being left alone in waking life. Psychologically, this dream could reflect unresolved issues from past relationships or childhood experiences. Spiritually, abandonment dreams may suggest a need to reconnect with one's inner self or spiritual path.

Abduction

Abduction dreams often symbolize feelings of powerlessness, being taken advantage of, or losing control over one's life. Psychologically, they may reflect fears of vulnerability or being overwhelmed by external forces. Spiritually, abduction could represent a call to reclaim personal power or face hidden fears.

Accident

Dreaming of an accident often reflects fears of unexpected change or loss of control. Experiencing an accident in a dream might indicate concerns about safety or fear of making mistakes. Psychologically, it can represent anxiety or worries about potential failures. Spiritually, it may signify a need to address underlying fears or seek guidance in managing life's unpredictabilities.

Adventure

An adventure dream typically represents a desire for excitement, change, or a break from routine. Psychologically, it could indicate a need to challenge oneself or take risks. Spiritually, it might suggest a journey towards self-discovery or exploring new spiritual horizons.

Aeroplane

Aeroplanes in dreams often symbolize the desire for escape, freedom, or a change in perspective. **Flying in an aeroplane** might suggest the pursuit of new opportunities or a higher perspective on a situation, while **crashing in an aeroplane** could indicate fears or anxieties about an undertaking or significant life changes. Psychologically, aeroplanes represent the mind's desire to transcend limitations or gain a broader view. Spiritually, they may signify ascension, the connection to higher realms, or the pursuit of spiritual enlightenment.

Airport

Airports in dreams typically symbolize transitions, new beginnings, or a journey. Psychologically, they may represent anticipation or anxiety about change. Spiritually, an airport could indicate readiness for a new phase of life or the start of a spiritual journey.

Amber

Amber in dreams often symbolizes warmth, energy, and change. Seeing amber might indicate a need for balance and positivity, or suggest upcoming transformations. Psychologically, it represents the influence of optimism and vitality. Spiritually, it may signify divine encouragement to embrace change and find joy in life's transitions.

Amethyst

Amethyst in dreams often symbolizes spiritual growth, intuition, and clarity. Seeing amethyst can indicate that you are developing a deeper understanding of yourself or that you are experiencing heightened spiritual awareness. It may also suggest the need for calm and peace, as amethyst is known for its calming and healing properties.

Amputation

Dreaming of amputation can symbolize feelings of loss, helplessness, or being cut off from something important. Psychologically, it might reflect fears of losing one's abilities or identity. Spiritually, it could signify the need to let go of something that no longer serves you or the process of releasing past attachments.

Angels

Angels in dreams often symbolize protection, guidance, or a connection to the divine. Psychologically, they might reflect a need for comfort, hope, or reassurance. Spiritually, angels can represent messengers from the divine or symbols of spiritual enlightenment.

Animals

Animals in dreams can represent instincts, emotions, and the more primal aspects of our nature. The specific animal often provides additional insight:

Dogs may symbolize loyalty, friendship, or protection.

Cats can represent independence, intuition, or mystery.

Snakes often symbolize transformation, healing, or hidden fears.

Anniversary

Dreaming of an anniversary typically reflects reflection on past relationships or significant milestones. Celebrating an anniversary might indicate a desire to revisit past successes or relationships, while missing an anniversary could suggest feelings of regret or unresolved issues from the past. Psychologically, it represents a focus on important events and personal milestones. Spiritually, it may signify the need to acknowledge and celebrate life's significant moments or resolve lingering concerns.

Ants

Ants in dreams often symbolise industriousness, teamwork, or the handling of small but numerous tasks. **Seeing ants** might suggest the need to address minor but persistent issues or to recognise the value of hard work and collaboration. **Being overwhelmed by ants** could indicate feeling burdened by too many small problems or a lack of personal space. Psychologically, ants represent the mind's focus on diligence, the importance of small tasks, and collective effort. Spiritually, they might signify the significance of unity, the rewards of hard work, or the power of persistence.

Apple

Apples in dreams often symbolise knowledge, temptation, or abundance. **Eating an apple** might suggest a desire for knowledge, the enjoyment of life's pleasures, or the temptation of something forbidden. **Seeing a rotten apple** could indicate the presence of decay or dissatisfaction with something in your life. Psychologically, apples represent the mind's pursuit of knowledge, the experience of temptation, or the enjoyment of abundance. Spiritually, they may signify divine wisdom, the temptation of the forbidden, or the manifestation of spiritual abundance.

Aquarium

Aquariums in dreams often symbolise containment, observation, or the need to explore one's emotions. **Looking at fish in an aquarium** might suggest the desire to observe or understand emotions or situations in a controlled environment, while **seeing a cracked aquarium** could indicate feelings of vulnerability or the fear of losing control. Psychologically, aquariums represent the mind's focus on emotional observation, containment, or the need to address repressed feelings. Spiritually, they may signify the need to explore inner depths, the preservation of spiritual insights, or the containment of sacred experiences.

Armadillo

Armadillos in dreams often symbolise protection, boundaries, or the need to shield oneself. **Seeing an armadillo** might suggest a need to protect yourself from emotional harm or to set boundaries, while **interacting with an armadillo** could indicate the desire for security or the need to address defensive behaviours. Psychologically, armadillos represent the mind's focus on self-protection, boundary-setting, and the management of emotional safety. Spiritually, they may signify the need for spiritual protection, the importance of boundaries, or the shielding of sacred aspects of the self.

Aqua

Aqua, a blend of blue and green, often symbolizes tranquillity, healing, and emotional balance. Dreaming of aqua might suggest a need for calmness or indicate that emotional healing is underway. Psychologically, it represents a desire for peace and emotional stability. Spiritually, it may signify divine support in achieving inner harmony and renewal.

B

Babies

Dreaming of babies often signifies new beginnings, innocence, or vulnerability. Psychologically, it might reflect a desire to nurture or be nurtured, the early stages of a new project or idea, or the need for care and attention. **Seeing a baby** could suggest the birth of a new idea, a desire for nurturing, or the need to address unresolved issues from childhood. **Caring for a baby** might indicate a need to nurture aspects of yourself or others, while **seeing a baby in distress** could reflect concerns about vulnerability or the need for protection. Spiritually, babies can represent purity, potential, the presence of divine innocence, or a fresh start in one's spiritual journey, including the nurturing of spiritual potential.

Ball

Balls in dreams often symbolise playfulness, opportunities, or the pursuit of goals. **Playing with a ball** might suggest a need for enjoyment, relaxation, or the pursuit of personal goals, while **losing a ball** could indicate missed opportunities or challenges in achieving your desires. Psychologically, balls represent the mind's focus on play, the pursuit of goals, or the enjoyment of life's pleasures. Spiritually, they may signify the flow of energy, the manifestation of desires, or the presence of divine opportunities.

Balloons

Balloons in dreams often symbolize hopes, dreams, or a desire to rise above difficulties. A rising balloon might suggest optimism or the lifting of burdens, while a deflating balloon could reflect disappointment or unfulfilled expectations. Psychologically, balloons can represent aspirations or the fragility of dreams.

Spiritually, they might signify the soul's ascent or the release of negative energies.

Bee

Bees in dreams often symbolise hard work, community, or the sweet rewards of effort. **Seeing a bee** might suggest the value of industriousness, the importance of community, or the sweetness of life's rewards, while **being stung by a bee** could indicate feelings of hurt or the consequences of overexertion. Psychologically, bees represent the mind's focus on productivity, the importance of collective effort, and the rewards of hard work. Spiritually, they may signify divine guidance, the sweetness of spiritual abundance, or the interconnectedness of the soul.

Bird

Birds in dreams often symbolise freedom, aspiration, or the ability to rise above challenges. **Seeing a bird** might suggest a desire for freedom or a need to take a broader perspective on a situation, while **being attacked by a bird** could indicate feelings of vulnerability or threats. Psychologically, birds represent the mind's focus on freedom, aspiration, and the overcoming of obstacles. Spiritually, they may signify divine guidance, the elevation of the soul, or the manifestation of spiritual aspirations.

Birthday

Dreams about birthdays often symbolise personal growth, milestones, or a new phase in life. Celebrating your own birthday might indicate a sense of achievement or a readiness for change, while attending someone else's birthday could reflect feelings about your relationship with that person. Psychologically, birthdays represent self-reflection and the marking of life's stages. Spiritually, they may signify divine blessings or new beginnings.

Black

Black in dreams often symbolises the unknown, mystery, or aspects of the self that are hidden. Seeing black might reflect fears or anxieties about the unknown or signify the need to explore unconscious aspects of your life. Psychologically, it represents the exploration of hidden fears and unresolved issues. Spiritually, it may signify divine guidance in confronting and understanding your deeper self.

Blood

Blood in dreams often symbolizes life force, energy, or passion. Seeing blood might suggest a vital energy or a deep emotional wound, while losing blood could indicate feeling drained or weakened. Psychologically, blood can represent emotional or physical health. Spiritually, it might signify the essence of life, sacrifice, or spiritual vitality.

Blue

Blue in dreams often symbolises calmness, trust, and communication. Dreaming of blue might indicate a need for peace or a focus on improving communication. Psychologically, it represents the desire for emotional stability and clear expression. Spiritually, it may signify divine reassurance and guidance towards maintaining balance and trust in your journey.

Books

Books in dreams often symbolize knowledge, wisdom, or the desire to learn. Reading a book might indicate a search for understanding or guidance, while an unread book could reflect untapped potential or unexplored aspects of oneself. Psychologically, books can represent the mind's quest for knowledge. Spiritually, they might signify sacred texts or divine wisdom.

Boxes

Boxes in dreams often symbolize secrets, hidden aspects of oneself, or things yet to be discovered. Opening a box might suggest revealing something hidden or discovering new opportunities, while a closed box could indicate something being kept from you or a mystery. Psychologically, boxes can represent the mind's way of compartmentalizing thoughts or emotions.

Spiritually, they may symbolize hidden truths or divine gifts.

Breakup

Dreaming of a breakup often signifies emotional distress or the end of a significant relationship. Experiencing a breakup might reflect feelings of loss, rejection, or the need to let go of a relationship or situation. Psychologically, it represents unresolved emotions or fears of separation. Spiritually, it may signify the need to release old attachments or seek healing and closure.

Bridge

Bridges in dreams often symbolise transitions, connections, or the ability to overcome obstacles. **Crossing a bridge** might suggest a transition between different phases of life or the ability to overcome challenges, while **seeing a broken bridge** could indicate obstacles or difficulties in making a connection. Psychologically, bridges represent the mind's focus on transitions, connections, and overcoming challenges. Spiritually, they may signify the journey between different realms, the connection between the physical and spiritual, or the ability to bridge gaps in understanding.

C

Career Change

Dreams about a career change often symbolise transformation, personal growth, or new opportunities. Dreaming of changing jobs might indicate a desire for new challenges or the need to reassess your current path. Psychologically, it represents shifts in your identity or goals. Spiritually, it may signify divine guidance towards new directions or growth.

Car

Cars in dreams often symbolise personal direction, control, or the journey of life. **Driving a car** might suggest control over your life's direction or the pursuit of personal goals, while **being in a car accident** could indicate obstacles or challenges in your path. Psychologically, cars represent the mind's focus on direction, control, and personal progress. Spiritually, they may signify the journey of the soul, the pursuit of spiritual goals, or the navigation of life's challenges.

Cat

Cats in dreams often symbolise independence, intuition, or mystery. **Seeing a cat** might suggest a need for independence or the presence of intuition, while **being scratched by a cat** could indicate feelings of betrayal or the need to address unresolved issues. Psychologically, cats represent the mind's focus on independence, intuition, and mystery. Spiritually, they may signify the presence of spiritual insight, the need for personal freedom, or the exploration of the unknown.

Caves

Caves in dreams often symbolise the subconscious mind, hidden fears, or a place of retreat. **Exploring a cave** might suggest delving into one's inner self or confronting hidden emotions, while **being lost in a cave** could indicate feelings of confusion or being trapped in the subconscious. Psychologically, caves can represent the mind's hidden depths. Spiritually, they may symbolise a place of initiation, inner wisdom, or connection to the earth.

Chase

Being chased in a dream can signify feelings of anxiety, stress, or fear in waking life. Psychologically, it often reflects a situation or emotion one is avoiding. Spiritually, a chase dream might indicate that you are running from a truth or spiritual lesson that needs to be faced.

Childbirth

Dreams about childbirth often symbolise the birth of new ideas, projects, or aspects of yourself. **Giving birth in a dream** might represent creativity, personal growth, or the beginning of a new phase in life. Psychologically, it reflects a desire to create or nurture something new. Spiritually, it may signify divine blessings and the manifestation of new potential.

Citrine (Crystal/Mineral)

Citrine in dreams represents abundance, success, and personal power. Dreaming of citrine might suggest that you are on the path to achieving your goals or that you are attracting prosperity into your life. It can also signify confidence and the ability to manifest your desires through positive thinking and action.

Clear Skies

Clear skies in dreams often symbolize clarity, peace, and optimism. They reflect a period of calm, smooth progress, and positive outcomes. Dreaming of clear skies may indicate that you are in a favorable situation or that you are experiencing a time of emotional stability and personal growth.

Clear Quartz (Crystal/Mineral)

Clear quartz symbolizes clarity, amplification, and healing. In dreams, clear quartz can suggest a need for mental or emotional clarity and the power to enhance your personal energy. It may indicate that you are in a period of self-discovery or that you need to clear away confusion to see things more clearly.

Climbing

Climbing in dreams often symbolises ambition, striving for success, or personal growth. **Climbing a mountain** might suggest overcoming obstacles or reaching for higher goals, while **struggling to climb** could reflect challenges or fears of failure. Psychologically, climbing can represent the pursuit of one's aspirations. Spiritually, it might signify ascension, enlightenment, or the journey toward a higher state of being.

Cloud

Clouds in dreams often symbolise confusion, change, or the ethereal nature of thoughts. **Seeing clouds** might suggest a lack of clarity or the presence of change, while **seeing a clear sky** could indicate resolution or a clearer perspective. Psychologically, clouds represent the mind's focus on confusion, change, and the ethereal nature of thoughts. Spiritually, they may signify divine presence, the flow of spiritual energy, or the transition between different states of consciousness.

Coat

Coats in dreams often symbolise protection, identity, or the need for comfort. **Wearing a coat** might suggest a desire for protection or the need to present yourself in a certain way, while **losing a coat** could indicate feelings of vulnerability or a lack of comfort. Psychologically, coats represent the mind's focus on protection, identity, and comfort. Spiritually, they may signify the protection of the soul, the expression of spiritual identity, or the need for spiritual comfort.

Coffin

A coffin in a dream often symbolises endings, transformation, or the containment of something. **Seeing a coffin** might suggest the need to let go of something or someone, while **being inside a coffin** could indicate feelings of entrapment or fear of death. Psychologically, a coffin can represent the mind's way of dealing with the concept of mortality. Spiritually, it might signify rebirth, resurrection, or the cycle of life and death.

Colours
See specific colours

Crown
Crowns in dreams often symbolise authority, self-worth, or recognition. **Wearing a crown** might suggest feelings of achievement, recognition, or personal authority, while **losing a crown** could indicate feelings of diminished self-worth or loss of control. Psychologically, crowns represent the mind's focus on authority, self-worth, and recognition. Spiritually, they may signify divine approval, the recognition of spiritual achievements, or the embodiment of spiritual authority.

Crying
Crying in dreams often symbolises emotional release, grief, or the need for healing. **Crying uncontrollably** might suggest feelings of being overwhelmed or unresolved sadness, while **seeing someone else cry** could reflect empathy or concern for others. Psychologically, crying can represent the mind's way of processing emotions. Spiritually, it might signify purification, release of negative energies, or a call for emotional renewal.

Crimson
Crimson, a deep red, often symbolises passion, intensity, and power. Dreaming of crimson might reflect strong emotions or desires, or signify a need to assert yourself. Psychologically, it represents the focus on deep passions and energetic pursuits. Spiritually, it may signify divine encouragement to embrace your inner strength and pursue your goals with intensity.

Cyan

Cyan, a bright blue-green, often symbolises creativity, freshness, and clarity. Seeing cyan might indicate a need for creative expression or suggest that new ideas are emerging. Psychologically, it represents the focus on innovative thinking and clear communication. Spiritually, it may signify divine inspiration and guidance in pursuing creative or spiritual paths.

Isobel Chaucer

D

Dancing

Dancing in dreams often symbolizes joy, freedom, or the expression of emotions. Dancing alone might suggest self-expression or contentment, while dancing with others could indicate social connections or harmony. Psychologically, dancing can represent the mind's way of expressing feelings or desires. Spiritually, it might signify celebration, divine connection, or the dance of life itself.

Darkness

Darkness in dreams can symbolize the unknown, fear, or uncertainty. Psychologically, it might reflect feelings of confusion, depression, or being lost. Spiritually, darkness could represent a period of introspection or the 'dark night of the soul,' a phase of spiritual crisis or profound transformation.

Death

Dreams about death are often not literal but symbolic of change, transformation, or the end of a phase. Psychologically, they might reflect fear of the unknown or a desire for renewal. Spiritually, death dreams could represent a metaphorical dying of the old self and a rebirth into a new state of consciousness or understanding.

Desert

Deserts in dreams often symbolize isolation, desolation, or a spiritual journey. Wandering in a desert might suggest feelings of loneliness, searching for meaning, or being lost in life, while finding an oasis could indicate hope, relief, or spiritual nourishment. Psychologically, deserts can represent the mind's sense of barrenness or lack of emotional resources. Spiritually, they might signify a period of testing, purification, or spiritual awakening.

Diamonds

Diamonds in dreams often symbolize value, purity, or strength. Finding a diamond might suggest discovering inner strength or recognizing one's worth, while losing a diamond could reflect fears of losing something valuable or self-worth. Psychologically, diamonds can represent the mind's focus on what is precious or enduring. Spiritually, they might signify clarity, spiritual truth, or the indestructible nature of the soul.

Divorce

Dreams about divorce often symbolize the end of a significant relationship or personal change. Experiencing a divorce in a dream might reflect feelings of separation, loss, or the need to let go of certain aspects of your life. Psychologically, it represents a focus on emotional detachment or transition. Spiritually, it may signify the need for personal or spiritual realignment and the release of old connections.

Dolphin

Dolphins in dreams often symbolize intelligence, playfulness, or communication. **Seeing a dolphin** might suggest the need for joy, the presence of intelligent insight, or improved communication, while **being attacked by a dolphin** could indicate feelings of betrayal or the need to address issues in communication. Psychologically, dolphins represent the mind's focus on intelligence, playfulness, and communication. Spiritually, they may signify divine wisdom, the importance of joy, or the enhancement of spiritual communication.

Dog

Dogs in dreams often symbolise loyalty, protection, or companionship. **Seeing a dog** might suggest the presence of a loyal friend or the need for protection, while **being bitten by a dog** could indicate feelings of betrayal or a threat from someone you trust. Psychologically, dogs represent the mind's focus on loyalty, protection, and companionship. Spiritually, they may signify divine protection, the presence of spiritual guidance, or the importance of loyalty and trust.

Door

Doors in dreams often symbolise opportunities, transitions, or barriers. **Opening a door** might suggest new opportunities or transitions in your life, while **seeing a locked door** could indicate obstacles or barriers to progress. Psychologically, doors represent the mind's focus on opportunities, transitions, and barriers. Spiritually, they may signify the opening of new spiritual pathways, the transition between different realms, or the removal of obstacles to spiritual growth.

Dragon

Dragons in dreams often symbolise power, transformation, or hidden fears. **Seeing a dragon** might suggest the presence of powerful forces or the need to confront hidden fears, while **fighting a dragon** could indicate challenges or the need for personal transformation. Psychologically, dragons represent the mind's focus on power, transformation, and hidden fears. Spiritually, they may signify the presence of divine power, the process of spiritual transformation, or the need to confront deep-seated fears.

Dress

Dresses in dreams often symbolise identity, self-expression, or the roles we play. **Wearing a dress** might suggest the expression of your identity or the roles you assume, while **seeing a dress that doesn't fit** could indicate feelings of inadequacy or discomfort with your role. Psychologically, dresses represent the mind's focus on identity, self-expression, and the roles we play. Spiritually, they may signify the expression of spiritual identity, the manifestation of divine roles, or the alignment of the self with spiritual purpose

Drowning

Drowning in dreams often symbolizes overwhelming emotions, fears of being consumed, or losing control. **Struggling to stay afloat** might suggest dealing with emotional turmoil, while **sinking underwater** could indicate feeling overwhelmed by unconscious fears or repressed emotions. Psychologically, drowning can represent the mind's struggle with intense emotions or situations. Spiritually, it might signify a need for surrender, letting go, or a deep dive into the subconscious.

E

Eating

Eating in a dream can symbolize nourishment, satisfaction, or a desire to consume knowledge or experiences. The type of food and the context of the eating are important. Psychologically, eating could represent emotional needs or cravings, while spiritually, it might signify the assimilation of new wisdom or spiritual energy.

Eclipse

An eclipse in dreams often symbolizes obscured truths, hidden aspects, or a temporary loss of clarity. Seeing a solar eclipse might suggest feeling overshadowed or a significant change, while a lunar eclipse could indicate emotional shifts or inner transformation. Psychologically, eclipses can represent the mind's perception of blocked emotions or thoughts. Spiritually, they might signify the darkening before enlightenment, the temporary concealment of the divine, or a significant shift in consciousness.

Egg

Eggs in dreams often symbolize potential, new beginnings, or fragility. **Seeing an egg** might suggest the presence of new opportunities or potential, while **seeing a broken egg** could indicate the loss of potential or fragility in a situation. Psychologically, eggs represent the mind's focus on potential, new beginnings, and fragility. Spiritually, they may signify the birth of new spiritual insights, the manifestation of divine potential, or the protection of sacred beginnings.

Elephant

Elephants in dreams often symbolize wisdom, strength, or memory. **Seeing an elephant** might suggest the presence of wisdom or the need to remember important aspects of your life, while **being chased by an elephant** could indicate feelings of being overwhelmed by issues from the past. Psychologically, elephants represent the mind's focus on wisdom, strength, and memory. Spiritually, they may signify divine guidance, the manifestation of spiritual strength, or the importance of remembering spiritual lessons.

Engagement

Dreams about engagement often symbolize commitment, relationships, or the anticipation of future events. Being engaged in a dream might reflect feelings of readiness for a deeper commitment or a desire to solidify a relationship. Psychologically, it represents the anticipation of future changes or the need for deeper connections. Spiritually, it may signify divine affirmation or the alignment of personal and spiritual goals.

Escalator

Escalators in dreams often symbolize progress, transitions, or the ease of moving between different levels. **Riding an escalator** might suggest smooth progress or transitions in your life, while **being stuck on an escalator** could indicate feelings of stagnation or difficulty in making progress. Psychologically, escalators represent the mind's focus on progress, transitions, and the ease of moving between different levels. Spiritually, they may signify the smooth transition between spiritual realms, the progress of the soul, or the ease of spiritual advancement.

Exams

Dreaming of exams often symbolizes self-evaluation, stress, or the need to prove oneself. Taking an exam might reflect feelings of inadequacy or the pressure to meet expectations, while failing an exam could indicate fears of failure or self-doubt. Psychologically, it represents a focus on performance and achievement.

Spiritually, it may signify a test of faith or divine challenges in personal growth.

Explosion

Explosions in dreams often symbolize repressed emotions, sudden realizations, or destructive forces. **Witnessing an explosion** might suggest a sudden release of pent-up feelings or a shocking revelation, while **being caught in an explosion** could indicate feeling overwhelmed by external forces or internal turmoil. Psychologically, explosions can represent the mind's response to suppressed emotions or conflicts. Spiritually, they might signify a breakthrough, the destruction of old beliefs, or the explosive force of transformation.

Eyes

Eyes in dreams are often associated with perception, insight, and awareness. **Seeing clearly** can symbolize understanding or enlightenment, while **blurry vision** might reflect confusion or denial. Psychologically, eyes can represent a need to 'see' something clearly in waking life. Spiritually, they may symbolize the third eye or inner vision.

Isobel Chaucer

F

Falling

Falling in dreams often represents a loss of control, fear of failure, or feeling unsupported. Psychologically, it might reflect anxiety about a particular situation in waking life. Spiritually, falling can symbolize a descent into deeper aspects of the self or the need to ground oneself more firmly in reality.

Family Reunion

Dreams about family reunions often symbolize connection, reconciliation, or the need to address family dynamics. **Attending a family reunion** might reflect desires for connection or unresolved family issues, while **missing a reunion** could indicate feelings of estrangement or regret. Psychologically, it represents the need to resolve family conflicts or reconnect with loved ones. Spiritually, it may signify divine healing and the importance of family bonds.

Fire

Fire in dreams often symbolizes transformation, passion, or destruction. **Seeing a fire** might suggest burning away old habits or intense emotions, while **being consumed by fire** could indicate feelings of anger, guilt, or danger. Psychologically, fire can represent the mind's focus on purification or a need for change. Spiritually, it might signify the flame of enlightenment, divine inspiration, or the destructive force necessary for renewal.

Fish

Fish in dreams often symbolize abundance, emotions, or transformation. **Seeing fish** might suggest the presence of abundance or the exploration of emotions, while **catching a fish** could indicate the attainment of goals or the discovery of hidden aspects of yourself. Psychologically, fish represent the mind's focus on abundance, emotions, and transformation. Spiritually, they may signify divine blessings, the exploration of spiritual depths, or the manifestation of spiritual potential.

Flood

Floods in dreams often symbolize overwhelming emotions, unconscious fears, or a situation out of control. **Seeing a flood** might suggest feeling overwhelmed by emotions or circumstances, while **being swept away** by a flood could indicate a loss of control or feeling consumed by external pressures. Psychologically, floods can represent the mind's struggle with intense feelings or situations. Spiritually, they might signify purification, the cleansing of old energies, or a powerful emotional release.

Flower

Flowers in dreams often symbolize beauty, growth, or the expression of emotions. Seeing a flower might suggest the presence of beauty or the blossoming of new aspects of your life, while seeing a wilted flower could indicate feelings of decay or dissatisfaction. Psychologically, flowers represent the mind's focus on beauty, growth, and emotional expression. Spiritually, they may signify the manifestation of spiritual beauty, the growth of the soul, or the expression of divine emotions.

Flying

Flying in dreams often symbolizes freedom, transcendence, or the desire to rise above challenges. **Flying effortlessly** might suggest a sense of empowerment or liberation, while **struggling to fly** could indicate difficulties in achieving goals or overcoming obstacles. Psychologically, flying can represent the mind's aspirations or the need to escape from reality. Spiritually, it might signify ascension, the soul's journey, or a connection to higher consciousness.

Fog

Fog generally symbolizes confusion, lack of direction, or

obscured vision. In dreams, fog indicates mental or emotional blockages and a need for greater clarity. It suggests that you might be struggling to see things as they truly are or that you need to find your way through a period of uncertainty.

Forest

Forests in dreams often symbolize the subconscious mind, unknown territories, or a journey of self-discovery. **Wandering in a dense forest** might suggest feeling lost or exploring the depths of one's psyche, while **finding a path** through the forest could indicate gaining clarity or direction. Psychologically, forests can represent the mind's exploration of hidden aspects or unresolved issues. Spiritually, they might signify a place of initiation, the mysteries of life, or a connection to nature's wisdom.

Funeral

Dreams about funerals often symbolize closure, grief, or the end of a significant phase. **Attending a funeral** might reflect feelings of loss or the need to process grief, while **planning a funeral** could indicate the need to acknowledge an ending or closure. Psychologically, it represents the process of letting go or coming to terms with change. Spiritually, it may signify divine assistance in navigating grief and finding peace.

Isobel Chaucer

G

Garden

Gardens in dreams often symbolize growth, fertility, or the cultivation of ideas. **Tending to a garden** might suggest nurturing personal or spiritual growth, while a **neglected garden** could indicate missed opportunities or stagnation. Psychologically, gardens can represent the mind's focus on creativity or the need for self-care. Spiritually, they might signify paradise, the cultivation of virtues, or a space for meditation and inner peace.

Ghost

Ghosts in dreams often symbolize unresolved issues, lingering fears, or the past haunting the present. **Seeing a ghost** might suggest confronting past experiences or feelings of guilt, while **being chased by a ghost** could indicate fear of facing unresolved emotions. Psychologically, ghosts can represent the mind's attempt to deal with unfinished business. Spiritually, they might signify the presence of spirits, messages from the beyond, or the need to release past attachments.

Giant

Giants in dreams often symbolize overwhelming obstacles, power, or authority. **Facing a giant** might suggest confronting a major challenge or fear, while **being a giant** could indicate a sense of power or dominance. Psychologically, giants can represent the mind's perception of insurmountable problems or external pressures. Spiritually, they might signify a powerful force within, the need to confront one's inner demons, or the presence of a larger-than-life energy.

Giraffe

Giraffes in dreams often symbolize perspective, grace, or reaching for goals. **Seeing a giraffe** might suggest the need to elevate your perspective or the desire to achieve lofty goals, while **interacting with a giraffe** could indicate the need for grace or the ability to see beyond immediate concerns. Psychologically, giraffes represent the mind's focus on perspective, grace, and ambition. Spiritually, they may signify divine guidance, the elevation of the soul, or the pursuit of spiritual aspirations.

Glass

Glass in dreams often symbolizes transparency, fragility, or barriers. **Seeing through glass** might suggest clarity or insight, while **broken glass** could indicate shattered illusions, vulnerability, or the need to protect oneself. Spiritually, glass can represent a barrier to higher understanding or the fragility of the ego.

Glasses

Glasses in dreams often symbolize clarity, insight, or the need to see things more clearly. **Wearing glasses** might suggest the need for greater clarity or insight into a situation, while losing or **breaking glasses** could indicate difficulties in seeing or understanding things. Psychologically, glasses represent the mind's focus on clarity, insight, and the need for better vision. Spiritually, they may signify divine insight, the pursuit of spiritual clarity, or the enhancement of spiritual perception.

Glove

Gloves in dreams often symbolize protection, preparation, or the need to handle delicate situations. **Wearing gloves** might suggest the need for protection or preparation, while **losing or seeing damaged gloves** could indicate feelings of vulnerability or unpreparedness. Psychologically, gloves represent the mind's focus on protection, preparation, and handling delicate situations. Spiritually, they may signify the need for spiritual protection, the preparation for divine tasks, or the handling of sacred matters with care.

Gold

Gold in dreams often symbolizes wealth, success, and spiritual enlightenment. Seeing gold might reflect aspirations for prosperity or spiritual growth. Psychologically, it represents the pursuit of high ideals and personal success. Spiritually, it may signify divine recognition of your efforts and guidance towards achieving your highest potential.

Grave

Graves in dreams often symbolize endings, burial of the past, or contemplation of mortality. **Seeing a grave** might suggest the need to let go of something or reflect on the past, while **digging a grave** could indicate feelings of guilt or preparation for a significant change. Psychologically, graves can represent the mind's way of dealing with loss or unresolved issues. Spiritually, they might signify the cycle of life and death, the process of rebirth, or a deep connection to the earth.

Green

Green in dreams often symbolizes growth, renewal, and harmony. Dreaming of green might suggest personal growth or the need for healing. Psychologically, it represents a focus on renewal and balance. Spiritually, it may signify divine blessings and support in achieving harmony and progress in your life.

Guitar

Guitars in dreams often symbolize creativity, self-expression, or the desire to communicate. **Playing a guitar** might suggest the need for creative expression or the desire to communicate your feelings, while **seeing a broken guitar** could indicate difficulties in self-expression or the need to address creative blocks. Psychologically, guitars represent the mind's focus on creativity, self-expression, and communication. Spiritually, they may signify the manifestation of divine creativity, the expression of spiritual emotions, or the enhancement of spiritual communication.

Graduation

Dreams about graduation often symbolize achievement, transition, or the completion of a significant phase. Experiencing graduation in a dream might reflect a sense of accomplishment or readiness for new challenges. Psychologically, it represents the successful completion of a stage and the anticipation of new opportunities. Spiritually, it may signify divine recognition of your efforts and the readiness for spiritual growth.

Getting Lost

Dreams about getting lost often symbolize confusion, uncertainty, or the need for direction. Finding yourself lost in a dream might indicate feelings of being overwhelmed or uncertain about your path. Psychologically, it reflects a focus on navigating personal challenges or finding clarity. Spiritually, it may signify the need for divine guidance or the search for spiritual direction.

H

Hail

Hail represents sudden obstacles or harsh challenges. In dreams, hail signifies unexpected difficulties that may disrupt your plans or cause problems. It indicates a period where you might face abrupt and severe challenges, requiring resilience and adaptability.

Hair

Hair in dreams often symbolizes identity, strength, or vitality. **Cutting your hair** might suggest a desire for change or feeling a loss of power, while **long, flowing hair** could indicate confidence or freedom. Psychologically, hair can represent the mind's focus on self-image or personal power. Spiritually, it might signify a connection to one's roots, the flow of life energy, or the shedding of old layers.

Helicopter

Helicopters in dreams often symbolize high perspective, rapid change, or the ability to rise above challenges. **Riding in a helicopter** might suggest the ability to gain a higher perspective on a situation or to navigate rapid changes, while **seeing a helicopter crash** could indicate fears about loss of control or challenges in overcoming obstacles. Psychologically, helicopters represent the mind's focus on perspective, change, and overcoming challenges. Spiritually, they may signify divine guidance, the elevation of consciousness, or the ability to navigate spiritual challenges.

Hawk

Hawks in dreams often symbolize vision, focus, or the ability to see beyond the immediate. **Seeing a hawk** might suggest the need to gain a clearer perspective or to focus on your goals, while **being attacked by a hawk** could indicate the presence of aggressive forces or threats. Psychologically, hawks represent the mind's focus on vision, focus, and the ability to see beyond the immediate. Spiritually, they may signify divine insight, the elevation of spiritual vision, or the pursuit of higher spiritual goals.

Holiday

Dreams about holidays often symbolize relaxation, escape, or the need to take a break from routine. **Going on holiday** in a dream might reflect a desire for relaxation or a change of scenery, while **having difficulties during a holiday** could indicate challenges in finding peace or escape. Psychologically, it represents the need for rest and rejuvenation. Spiritually, it may signify divine support in finding balance or pursuing spiritual relaxation.

Horse

Horses in dreams often symbolize power, freedom, or the journey of life. **Riding a horse** might suggest the pursuit of personal freedom or the need to take control of your life's direction, while **seeing a wild horse** could indicate the presence of untamed energies or desires. Psychologically, horses represent the mind's focus on power, freedom, and the journey of life. Spiritually, they may signify divine guidance, the manifestation of spiritual power, or the pursuit of spiritual freedom.

House

Houses in dreams often symbolize the self, personal identity, or the different aspects of life. **Exploring a house** might suggest the need to explore different aspects of yourself or your life, while **seeing a house in disrepair** could indicate feelings of insecurity or unresolved issues. Psychologically, houses represent the mind's focus on self, identity, and the exploration of personal aspects. Spiritually, they may signify the exploration of the soul, the manifestation of divine identity, or the resolution of spiritual issues.

House Moving

Dreams about moving house often symbolize change, transition, or personal growth. Moving to a new house might reflect a desire for a fresh start or significant life changes, while struggling to move could indicate difficulties in managing transitions. Psychologically, it represents shifts in your life circumstances or identity. Spiritually, it may signify divine assistance in navigating changes or pursuing new beginnings.

Hospital

Hospitals in dreams often symbolize healing, recovery, or the need for care. **Being in a hospital** might suggest a need for physical, emotional, or spiritual healing, while **visiting someone in a hospital** could indicate concern for others or a desire to help. Psychologically, hospitals can represent the mind's focus on healing or addressing unresolved issues. Spiritually, they might signify a place of restoration, the process of spiritual renewal, or the need for self-care.

Hurricane

Hurricanes in dreams often symbolize overwhelming emotions, destructive forces, or sudden changes. **Being caught in a hurricane** might suggest feeling overwhelmed by life's challenges or intense emotions, while **watching a hurricane from a distance** could indicate fear of impending turmoil. Psychologically, hurricanes can represent the mind's response to chaos or stress. Spiritually, they might signify a powerful cleansing, a test of resilience, or the force of transformation.

Hug

Hugs in dreams often symbolize comfort, connection, or the need for emotional support. Receiving a hug might suggest the need for comfort or support, while giving a hug could indicate the desire to connect with others or to offer emotional support. Psychologically, hugs represent the mind's focus on comfort, connection, and emotional support. Spiritually, they may signify the presence of divine comfort, the connection of the soul, or the offering of spiritual support.

I

Ice

Ice in dreams often symbolizes coldness, emotional detachment, or obstacles. **Walking on ice** might suggest navigating a delicate situation or fear of losing control, while **melting ice** could indicate the thawing of emotions or the resolution of difficulties. Psychologically, ice can represent the mind's way of dealing with repressed emotions or challenges. Spiritually, it might signify a period of stillness, the process of emotional release, or the presence of hidden potentials.

Igloo

Igloos in dreams often symbolize protection, isolation, or the need for warmth and safety. **Being in an igloo** might suggest the need for protection or the desire for safety and warmth, while **seeing a damaged igloo** could indicate feelings of vulnerability or a lack of security. Psychologically, igloos represent the mind's focus on protection, isolation, and the need for safety. Spiritually, they may signify divine protection, the pursuit of spiritual warmth, or the need for security in sacred spaces.

Immigration

Dreams about immigration often symbolize transition, adaptation, or the desire for a fresh start. **Emigrating to a new country** might reflect a desire for change or a new beginning, while **experiencing difficulties with immigration** could indicate challenges in adapting to new circumstances. Psychologically, it represents the process of adapting to new environments or changes. Spiritually, it may signify divine guidance in finding your place or pursuing new opportunities.

Imprisonment

Imprisonment in dreams often symbolizes feelings of restriction, powerlessness, or being trapped. **Being in prison** might suggest feeling confined by circumstances or emotions, while **escaping from prison** could indicate a desire for freedom or overcoming limitations. Psychologically, imprisonment can represent the mind's struggle with limitations or control. Spiritually, it might signify the need to break free from negative patterns, the journey toward liberation, or the process of spiritual awakening.

Insect

Insects in dreams often symbolize minor issues, persistence, or the need to address small problems. **Seeing an insect** might suggest the presence of minor annoyances or the need to address small but persistent issues, while **being overwhelmed by insects** could indicate feelings of being burdened by numerous small problems. Psychologically, insects represent the mind's focus on minor issues, persistence, and the need to address small problems. Spiritually, they may signify the importance of addressing spiritual details, the persistence of divine guidance, or the management of small but significant aspects of the soul.

Invisible

Being invisible in dreams often symbolizes feelings of being overlooked, ignored, or disconnected from others. **Feeling invisible** might suggest a desire for recognition or a sense of not being seen or heard, while **making something invisible** could indicate a wish to hide or protect something. Psychologically, invisibility can represent the mind's response to feelings of insignificance or detachment. Spiritually, it might signify the presence of unseen forces, the desire for anonymity, or the exploration of non-physical realms.

Island

Islands in dreams often symbolize isolation, self-sufficiency, or the desire for solitude. **Being on an island** might suggest feelings of isolation or the need for self-sufficiency, while **seeing an island**

from afar could indicate the desire for solitude or the need to escape from a situation. Psychologically, islands represent the mind's focus on isolation, self-sufficiency, and solitude. Spiritually, they may signify the need for spiritual retreat, the pursuit of divine solitude, or the exploration of sacred spaces.

Indigo

Indigo, a deep blue-purple, often symbolizes intuition, wisdom, and higher consciousness. Dreaming of indigo might indicate a need to trust your intuition or suggest spiritual insights are emerging. Psychologically, it represents the focus on inner wisdom and intuitive understanding. Spiritually, it may signify divine guidance and support in connecting with your higher self.

Ivory

Ivory, a soft off-white, often symbolizes purity, calmness, and elegance. Seeing the colour ivory might suggest a desire for simplicity or a focus on purity in your life. Psychologically, it represents the need for clarity and refined qualities. Spiritually, it may signify divine grace and the importance of maintaining purity and balance in your spiritual journey.

Injury

Dreams about injury often symbolize vulnerability, pain, or the need to address emotional or physical issues. Sustaining an injury in a dream might reflect feelings of vulnerability or the need to address personal wounds. Psychologically, it represents concerns about your well-being or unresolved emotional issues. Spiritually, it may signify the need for healing or divine assistance in overcoming challenges.

J

Jade (Crystal/Mineral)

Jade in dreams often represents wisdom, balance, and harmony. Dreaming of jade might suggest that you are seeking or achieving balance in your life, or it could indicate that you are receiving or giving wise counsel. Jade is also associated with prosperity and good fortune, suggesting that positive changes are on the horizon.

Jaguar

Jaguars in dreams often symbolize power, stealth, or the need to confront primal instincts. **Seeing a jaguar** might suggest the presence of powerful forces or the need to address hidden aspects of yourself, while **being chased by a jaguar** could indicate fears of confronting primal instincts or aggressive forces. Psychologically, jaguars represent the mind's focus on power, stealth, and primal instincts. Spiritually, they may signify divine power, the manifestation of spiritual strength, or the need to confront deep-seated fears.

Jewellery

Jewellery in dreams can symbolize value, self-worth, or personal qualities. Gold jewellery might represent spiritual riches or wisdom, while silver jewellery could symbolize intuition, emotions, or feminine energy. Psychologically, losing jewellery might reflect fears of losing status or personal value.

Jewel

Jewels in dreams often symbolize value, beauty, or personal worth. **Seeing a jewel** might suggest the recognition of your value or the presence of beauty in your life, while **losing a jewel** could indicate feelings of diminished worth or the loss of something precious. Psychologically, jewels represent the mind's focus on value, beauty, and personal worth. Spiritually, they may signify divine worth, the manifestation of spiritual beauty, or the recognition of sacred value.

Jewel Box

A jewel box in dreams often symbolizes something valuable or hidden within oneself. **Opening a jewel box** might suggest discovering hidden talents or truths, while a **locked jewel box** could indicate something kept secret or guarded. Psychologically, a jewel box can represent the mind's focus on protecting or uncovering something precious. Spiritually, it might signify the containment of spiritual wisdom, the treasures of the soul, or the protection of sacred knowledge.

Jigsaw Puzzle

Jigsaw puzzles in dreams often symbolize problem-solving, complexity, or the need to piece together different aspects of life. **Working on a jigsaw puzzle** might suggest the need to solve complex problems or to integrate various aspects of your life, while **seeing incomplete pieces** could indicate feelings of frustration or the need to address unresolved issues. Psychologically, jigsaw puzzles represent the mind's focus on problem-solving, complexity, and integration. Spiritually, they may signify the need to piece together spiritual insights, the resolution of divine puzzles, or the integration of sacred aspects of the soul.

Jet

Jets in dreams often symbolize speed, ambition, or the desire to quickly achieve goals. **Riding in a jet** might suggest the need for rapid progress or the pursuit of ambitious goals, while **seeing a jet crash** could indicate fears about the potential for failure or the challenges in achieving your desires. Psychologically, jets represent the mind's focus on speed, ambition, and rapid progress. Spiritually, they may signify divine guidance in achieving spiritual goals, the pursuit of rapid spiritual advancement, or the overcoming of challenges in the journey of the soul.

Journey

Journeys in dreams often symbolize life's path, personal growth, or a quest for knowledge. **Embarking on a journey** might suggest a new phase in life or the pursuit of a goal, **while getting lost on a journey** could indicate uncertainty or fear of the future. Psychologically, journeys can represent the mind's way of processing change or development. Spiritually, they might signify the soul's quest for truth, the process of transformation, or the exploration of the unknown.

Jungle

Jungles in dreams often symbolize the unknown, complexity, or the need for exploration. **Being in a jungle** might suggest the exploration of unknown aspects of yourself or the need to navigate complex situations, while **being lost in a jungle** could indicate feelings of confusion or difficulty in finding your way. Psychologically, jungles represent the mind's focus on the unknown, complexity, and exploration. Spiritually, they may signify the exploration of spiritual mysteries, the navigation of complex spiritual paths, or the presence of divine guidance in the midst of confusion.

Jumping

Jumping in dreams often symbolizes taking a leap of faith, overcoming obstacles, or a desire for freedom. **Jumping from a height** might suggest courage in the face of challenges or a risky decision, while **failing to jump** could indicate fear of failure or hesitation. Psychologically, jumping can represent the mind's readiness to take action or move forward. Spiritually, it might signify a leap in consciousness, the crossing of thresholds, or the act of surrendering to the unknown.

Job Interview

Dreams about job interviews often symbolize self-evaluation, opportunities, or the need to prove oneself. Participating in a job interview might reflect feelings of pressure to perform or a desire for new opportunities. Psychologically, it represents the focus on career advancement or self-worth. Spiritually, it may signify divine guidance in pursuing new paths or personal growth.

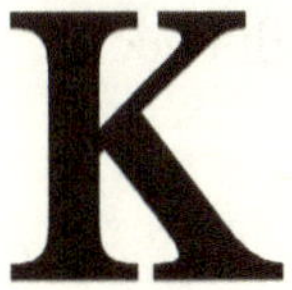

K

Kangaroo

Kangaroos in dreams often symbolize adaptability, movement, or the ability to overcome obstacles. **Seeing a kangaroo** might suggest the need to adapt to new situations or the ability to overcome challenges, while being **chased by a kangaroo** could indicate feelings of being overwhelmed by rapidly changing circumstances. Psychologically, kangaroos represent the mind's focus on adaptability, movement, and overcoming obstacles. Spiritually, they may signify divine guidance in navigating spiritual challenges, the manifestation of spiritual adaptability, or the pursuit of higher spiritual goals.

Key/Keys

Keys in dreams often symbolize access, solutions, or the unlocking of potential and opportunities. **Finding a key** might suggest discovering a solution or unlocking hidden potential, while **losing a key** could indicate feelings of frustration, helplessness, or barriers to progress. Psychologically, keys represent the mind's focus on access, control, and unlocking different aspects of one's life. Spiritually, they may signify divine access, entry into new levels of understanding, or the resolution of spiritual mysteries.

Kidnapping

Kidnapping in dreams often symbolizes feeling trapped, controlled, or forced into a situation. **Being kidnapped** might suggest feeling powerless or manipulated, while **witnessing a kidnapping** could indicate fear of losing control over a situation. Psychologically, kidnapping can represent the mind's response to feelings of entrapment or coercion. Spiritually, it might signify the need to reclaim one's power, the journey of liberation, or the struggle against external influences.

Killing

Killing in dreams often symbolizes the desire to end something, whether it be a habit, relationship, or aspect of oneself. **Killing an animal** might suggest suppressing instincts or desires, while **killing a person** could indicate a deep-seated anger or a need to eliminate certain behaviours. Psychologically, killing can represent the mind's attempt to deal with aggression, fear, or change. Spiritually, it might signify the death of the ego, the end of a cycle, or the necessity of transformation.

King

Kings in dreams often symbolize authority, power, or leadership. **Seeing a king** might suggest the presence of authority or the need to take on leadership roles, while **being dethroned** could indicate feelings of diminished power or loss of control. Psychologically, kings represent the mind's focus on authority, power, and leadership. Spiritually, they may signify divine authority, the manifestation of spiritual power, or the need to embrace spiritual leadership.

Knife/Knives

Knives in dreams often symbolize conflict, separation, or the need to cut through something. **Holding a knife** might suggest a desire for protection or the need to confront a situation, while **being attacked or threatened by a knife** could indicate feelings of vulnerability, fear, or betrayal. Psychologically, knives represent the mind's focus on defence, aggression, or the need to sever ties and cut out negative influences. Spiritually, they might signify the cutting away of illusions, the power of discernment, or the tool for spiritual surgery—removing impurities and revealing penetrating truths.

Kite

Kites in dreams often symbolize freedom, aspirations, or the pursuit of goals. **Flying a kite** might suggest the pursuit of personal goals or the desire for freedom, while **seeing a kite stuck in a tree** could indicate obstacles or challenges in achieving your aspirations. Psychologically, kites represent the mind's focus on freedom, aspirations, and the pursuit of goals. Spiritually, they may signify the elevation of the soul, the pursuit of divine aspirations, or the overcoming of spiritual obstacles.

Kissing

Kissing in dreams often represents affection, intimacy, or a desire for connection. **Kissing someone** in a dream might reflect feelings of affection or the need for closer relationships, while **being kissed unexpectedly** could indicate surprise or new connections. Psychologically, it can suggest a blending of qualities or a wish for union. Spiritually, kissing may symbolize the exchange of energy or a merging of souls

L

Labyrinth

Labyrinths in dreams often symbolize complexity, the journey of self-discovery, or the search for answers. **Navigating a labyrinth** might suggest exploring complex aspects of yourself or seeking answers, while **being lost in a labyrinth** could indicate feelings of confusion or difficulty finding your way. Psychologically, labyrinths represent the mind's focus on complexity and self-discovery. Spiritually, they signify the soul's journey, the exploration of spiritual mysteries, or divine guidance in navigating challenges.

Ladder

Ladders in dreams often symbolize progress, ascension, or the journey toward a goal. **Climbing a ladder** might suggest striving for success or spiritual growth, while **falling from a ladder** could indicate fear of failure or setbacks. Psychologically, ladders can represent ambition and steps needed to achieve goals. Spiritually, they signify the ascent to higher consciousness, the connection between different levels of existence, or spiritual evolution.

Lake

Lakes in dreams often symbolize emotions, reflection, or the subconscious mind. **A calm lake** might suggest inner peace or a period of reflection, while **a stormy lake** could indicate turbulent emotions or unresolved issues. Psychologically, lakes represent the mind's exploration of feelings or the need for introspection. Spiritually, they signify the depths of the soul, the mirror of the inner world, or hidden truths.

Lamp

Lamps in dreams often symbolize enlightenment, guidance, or the illumination of knowledge. **Seeing a lamp** might suggest a need for clarity or insights, while **a broken lamp** could indicate difficulties in gaining understanding. Psychologically, lamps represent enlightenment, guidance, and knowledge. Spiritually, they signify divine illumination, the pursuit of spiritual enlightenment, or the revelation of sacred insights.

Lapis Lazuli (Crystal/Mineral)
Lapis lazuli symbolizes truth, intuition, and spiritual insight. Seeing lapis lazuli in a dream can indicate that you are connecting with your higher self or seeking deeper truths. It may also suggest that you need to trust your intuition or express your authentic self more freely.

Lifts
A lift in a dream often symbolizes movement between different levels of consciousness or aspects of oneself. **Going up** in a lift might represent spiritual ascension, growth, or ambition, while **going down** could signify introspection, facing hidden fears, or exploring the subconscious mind.

Light
Light in dreams is often associated with clarity, understanding, or spiritual awakening. **A bright light** might symbolize divine presence, truth, or hope, while **a dim or flickering light** could indicate confusion or uncertainty. Psychologically, light represents insight or revelation. Spiritually, it signifies enlightenment, guidance, or higher consciousness.

Lion
Lions in dreams often symbolize power, courage, or leadership. **Facing a lion** might suggest confronting fears or asserting dominance, while **running from a lion** could indicate fear of confrontation or powerful challenges. Psychologically, lions represent strength, authority, and overcoming obstacles. Spiritually, they signify divine courage, spiritual strength, or

leadership.

Lightning

Lightning in dreams often symbolizes sudden insight, power, or destruction. **Seeing lightning** might suggest a sudden realization or powerful force, while **being struck by lightning** could indicate a life-changing event or burst of inspiration. Psychologically, lightning represents sudden changes or revelations. Spiritually, it signifies divine inspiration, transformation, or higher energy.

Lock

Locks in dreams often symbolize barriers, security, or the need to protect something valuable. **Seeing a lock** might suggest barriers or the need for protection, while **losing a key to a lock** could indicate difficulties in accessing or securing what is important. Psychologically, locks represent barriers and protection. Spiritually, they signify divine protection, the resolution of spiritual barriers, or unlocking sacred insights.

Lost

Dreams of being lost often reflect feelings of confusion, lack of direction, or insecurity. Being **lost in a familiar place** might suggest feeling out of touch with one's roots or true self, while being **lost in an unknown location** could indicate fear of the unknown or new experiences. Psychologically, these dreams point to a need for guidance or clarity. Spiritually, they represent a soul searching for purpose or direction.

Legal Issues

Dreams about legal issues often symbolize concerns about justice, responsibility, or personal boundaries. Facing legal problems in a dream might reflect anxieties about fairness or the need to address personal boundaries. Psychologically, it represents concerns about responsibility or legal matters. Spiritually, it signifies the need to seek divine justice or guidance in resolving conflicts.

Lavender

Dreams featuring the colour lavender often symbolize relaxation, spirituality, and healing. Lavender, a soft purple, is associated with calmness and spiritual growth. Seeing lavender in a dream might reflect a need for relaxation or spiritual connection. Psychologically, it represents soothing of the mind and emotions. Spiritually, it signifies divine healing, spiritual growth, and nurturing of the soul.

Lilac

Dreams involving the colour lilac often symbolize love, romance, and innocence. Lilac, a pale violet, represents youthful love and purity of emotions. Seeing lilac in a dream might reflect a desire for romantic connection or the purity of a new relationship. Psychologically, it represents gentle, nurturing aspects of love. Spiritually, it signifies divine love, innocence, and blossoming of spiritual connections.

Magenta

Magenta, a vibrant pink-purple, often symbolizes creativity, compassion, and transformation. Dreaming of magenta might reflect a desire for emotional expression or indicate personal transformation. Psychologically, it represents creative and emotional development. Spiritually, it signifies divine support in embracing change and pursuing passions.

Malachite (Crystal/Mineral)

Malachite in dreams represents transformation, healing, and protection. Dreaming of malachite might suggest that you are undergoing significant personal changes or healing from past wounds. It can also indicate a need for protection from negative influences or a call to embrace personal growth and transformation.

Maroon

Maroon, a dark red-brown, often symbolizes stability, ambition, and depth. Seeing maroon might indicate a focus on long-term goals or the need for grounding. Psychologically, it represents the pursuit of stability and ambition. Spiritually, it signifies divine encouragement to stay grounded and focused on deeper aspirations.

Maze

Mazes in dreams often symbolize confusion, complexity, or difficult situations. **Navigating a maze** might suggest trying to find a solution to a problem or dealing with confusion, while being **lost in a maze** could indicate feelings of being overwhelmed or trapped. Psychologically, mazes represent the mind's struggle with decision-making or finding a way forward. Spiritually, they signify the journey through life's complexities, the search for truth, or exploration of the subconscious mind.

Mirror

Mirrors in dreams often symbolize self-reflection, identity, or the desire for clarity. **Looking into a mirror** might suggest examining oneself or confronting the truth, while a **broken or distorted mirror** could indicate issues with self-image or difficulties in seeing things clearly. Psychologically, mirrors represent the mind's focus on self-perception and understanding. Spiritually, they signify the reflection of the soul, unveiling hidden truths, or the connection between physical and spiritual worlds.

Money

Money in dreams can symbolize value, power, or self-worth. **Finding money** might indicate new opportunities or gains, while **losing money** could reflect fears of loss or insecurity. Psychologically, money represents energy exchange or personal resources. Spiritually, it might symbolize lessons about abundance, generosity, or the material versus the spiritual.

Monsters

Monsters in dreams often represent fears, anxieties, or repressed emotions. **Facing a monster** might suggest confronting one's fears or inner demons, while **being chased by a monster** could indicate running from problems or unresolved issues. Psychologically, monsters can symbolize parts of the psyche that have been rejected or feared. Spiritually, they might represent spiritual challenges or tests on the path to enlightenment.

Mountain

Mountains in dreams often symbolize challenges, aspirations, or spiritual ascent. **Climbing a mountain** might suggest striving for a goal or spiritual growth, while **standing at the top** could indicate success or enlightenment. Psychologically, mountains represent the mind's focus on overcoming obstacles or achieving something significant. Spiritually, they signify the journey to higher consciousness, the presence of divine power, or the path to self-realization.

Moon

The moon in dreams often symbolizes emotions, intuition, or the cyclical nature of life. **A full moon** might suggest heightened emotions or clarity, while **a new moon** could indicate new beginnings or hidden potential. Psychologically, the moon represents the mind's connection to emotions, cycles, or the subconscious. Spiritually, it signifies the rhythm of life, the connection to the divine feminine, or the illumination of the inner world.

Mansion

Mansions in dreams often symbolize wealth, status, or different aspects of the self. **Exploring a mansion** might suggest examining various aspects of oneself or one's life, while seeing a **mansion in disrepair** could indicate feelings of insecurity or issues with status. Psychologically, mansions represent the mind's focus on wealth, status, and self. Spiritually, they signify the manifestation of divine abundance, exploration of spiritual aspects, or resolution of issues related to status and self.

Marriage

Dreams about marriage often symbolize commitment, union, or the blending of different aspects of oneself. Getting married in a dream might reflect desires for commitment or integration of different parts of your life. Psychologically, it represents the desire for connection or stability. Spiritually, it signifies divine approval or alignment of personal and spiritual goals.

Moonstone (Crystal/Mineral)

Moonstone symbolizes intuition, emotion, and new beginnings. In dreams, moonstone often suggests that you are in touch with your emotional and intuitive side or that you are beginning a new phase in your life. It may also indicate a need to pay attention to your feelings and to trust your inner guidance.

Moving

Dreams about moving often symbolize change, transition, or the need to adjust to new circumstances. **Moving to a new place** might reflect a desire for a fresh start or the need to adapt to new situations, while **struggling with the move** could indicate difficulties in managing change. Psychologically, it represents the process of adapting to life changes. Spiritually, it signifies divine support in navigating transitions or seeking new beginnings.

N

Nakedness

Nakedness in dreams often symbolizes vulnerability, exposure, or authenticity. **Being naked in public** might suggest feelings of insecurity or fear of judgment, while **feeling comfortable being naked** could indicate self-acceptance or freedom from societal norms. Psychologically, nakedness can represent the mind's focus on honesty or the fear of being exposed. Spiritually, it might signify the shedding of illusions, the embrace of one's true self, or the return to a pure, unconditioned state.

Nest

Nests in dreams often symbolize home, security, or nurturing. **Finding a nest** might suggest finding a safe place or the desire to create a home, while **a broken nest** could indicate feelings of insecurity or loss. Psychologically, nests can represent the mind's focus on safety, comfort, or the need to nurture something. Spiritually, they might signify the creation of a sacred space, the birth of new ideas, or the protection of something valuable.

Necklace

Necklaces in dreams often symbolize connection, value, or adornment. **Wearing a necklace** might suggest pride in one's achievements or the desire to express oneself, while **losing a necklace** could indicate feelings of loss or insecurity. Psychologically, necklaces can represent the mind's focus on personal identity or the desire to be seen. Spiritually, they might signify the connection between the physical and spiritual, the expression of inner beauty, or the presence of a protective charm.

Needle

Needles in dreams often symbolize precision, pain, or the need to address specific issues. **Seeing a needle** might suggest the need for precision or the presence of pain, while **being pricked by a needle** could indicate the need to address specific issues or challenges. Psychologically, needles represent the mind's focus on precision, pain, and specific issues. Spiritually, they may signify divine precision, the resolution of spiritual pain, or the addressing of sacred challenges.

Nectar

Nectar in dreams often symbolizes sweetness, nourishment, or the pursuit of spiritual fulfillment. **Seeing nectar** might suggest the presence of sweetness or nourishment in your life, while **drinking nectar** could indicate the pursuit of spiritual fulfilment or the enjoyment of divine blessings. Psychologically, nectar represents the mind's focus on sweetness, nourishment, and fulfilment. Spiritually, it may signify divine blessings, the pursuit of spiritual nourishment, or the enjoyment of sacred rewards.

Night

Night in dreams often symbolizes mystery, the unconscious, or introspection. **A dark night** might suggest feelings of fear or uncertainty, while **a starry night** could indicate hope, inspiration, or cosmic guidance. Psychologically, night can represent the unknown parts of the mind or the hidden aspects of oneself. Spiritually, it may symbolize a period of spiritual darkness or the 'dark night of the soul'—a phase of spiritual transformation.

Nightmare

Nightmares in dreams often symbolize fears, anxieties, or unresolved issues. **Experiencing a nightmare** might suggest the presence of deep-seated fears or unresolved issues in your life, while **waking up from a nightmare** could indicate the need to confront or address these fears. Psychologically, nightmares represent the mind's focus on fears, anxieties, and unresolved issues. Spiritually, they may signify the need for spiritual healing, the resolution of karmic issues, or the presence of divine guidance in confronting fears.

Numbers

Numbers in dreams can carry specific symbolic meanings, often reflecting personal significance, spiritual teachings, or psychological states.

One

Unity, new beginnings, individuality, and self.

Seeing the number one might symbolize a fresh start, the importance of self-reliance, or the need to focus on your personal goals. It could also reflect a sense of unity or a significant new phase in your life.

Two

Duality, balance, partnership, and relationships.

The number two often represents the need to address relationships or partnerships. It might suggest the importance of balance and harmony in your life or highlight dual aspects of a situation or your personality.

Three

Creativity, growth, completion, and the Trinity (mind, body, spirit).

Seeing the number three may indicate a time of creative expansion or personal growth. It often symbolizes the completion of a cycle or the alignment of different aspects of yourself or a situation.

Four

Stability, structure, foundation, and order.

The number four often represents stability and structure in your life. It could signify the need to create a solid foundation or address issues related to order and organization. It might also reflect the four elements or the need for balance.

Five

 Change, freedom, adventure, and dynamic energy.
Seeing the number five might indicate upcoming changes or the need for freedom and adventure. It could suggest that you're ready to embrace new experiences or that dynamic forces are at play in your life.

Six

Harmony, responsibility, family, and nurturing.
The number six often relates to themes of harmony and responsibility, particularly within family or domestic settings. It might reflect a need to nurture or take responsibility for certain aspects of your life.

Seven

Spiritual growth, intuition, introspection, and perfection.
The number seven is frequently associated with spiritual insight and intuition. It might suggest a period of introspection or the pursuit of spiritual goals. Seven can also indicate a sense of completeness or perfection.

Eight

Abundance, power, material success, and balance.
Seeing the number eight might represent material abundance or personal power. It often indicates a need to balance different aspects of your life, particularly those related to success and achievement.

Nine

Completion, humanitarianism, wisdom, and introspection.
The number nine often signifies the completion of a phase or project. It might also indicate a focus on humanitarian efforts or the acquisition of wisdom and insight. It can suggest that you're nearing the end of a significant journey.

Ten

Wholeness, new beginnings, and the culmination of cycles.

Seeing the number ten often symbolizes the end of a cycle and the beginning of a new one. It reflects the idea of wholeness and completion, suggesting that you are ready to embark on a new phase of your life.

Eleven

Intuition, enlightenment, and spiritual awakening.

The number eleven is often seen as a master number in numerology, symbolizing higher intuition and spiritual enlightenment. It might suggest that you're on the cusp of a significant spiritual awakening or that your intuitive abilities are heightened.

Twelve

Completion, cycles, and divine order.

The number twelve often signifies completion of cycles and divine order. It might relate to the completion of a significant phase or the alignment of various aspects of your life with a higher order.

Thirteen

Transformation, rebirth, and change.

Although sometimes considered unlucky, the number thirteen often symbolizes transformation and rebirth. It might suggest a period of significant change or a need to embrace a new beginning.

Twenty-Two

Mastery, manifesting dreams, and building strong foundations.

As another master number, twenty-two symbolizes the ability to manifest dreams into reality and build strong foundations. It might suggest that you are in a position to achieve significant goals or make substantial progress.

Thirty-Three
Compassion, spiritual guidance, and healing.
The number thirty-three often represents the highest form of spiritual guidance and compassion. It might indicate that you are receiving divine support or are called to offer compassion and healing to others.

Nursing
Dreams about nursing often symbolize care, healing, or the need to address emotional or physical needs. **Caring for someone** in a dream might reflect a desire to nurture or support, while **being nursed** could indicate a need for care or healing. Psychologically, it represents the focus on personal needs or the need to address vulnerabilities. Spiritually, it may signify divine support in healing or nurturing.

New Job
Dreams about starting a new job often symbolize change, opportunity, or personal growth. Beginning a new job in a dream might reflect excitement about new opportunities or the desire for career advancement. Psychologically, it represents the anticipation of change or growth in your professional life. Spiritually, it may signify divine guidance towards new paths or the pursuit of personal development.

O

Obligation

Dreams about obligations often symbolize responsibility, pressure, or the need to fulfil commitments. Facing obligations in a dream might reflect feelings of being overwhelmed or the need to address responsibilities. Psychologically, it represents the focus on duties or pressures. Spiritually, it may signify the need for divine assistance in managing responsibilities or finding balance.

Obsession

Dreams of obsession often reflect compulsive thoughts, desires, or fears that dominate the waking mind. Obsessing over a person or object in a dream might suggest unresolved issues or a need to let go. Psychologically, these dreams could indicate fixation or an inability to move forward. Spiritually, they may represent attachment or a warning against excessive attachment to worldly desires.

Obsidian

Obsidian in dreams often symbolizes protection, clarity, or transformation. Holding a piece of obsidian might suggest the need for protection or the desire to see the truth clearly, while seeing an obsidian mirror could indicate self-reflection or the unveiling of hidden aspects of oneself. Psychologically, obsidian can represent the mind's focus on protection from negativity or the need for clarity. Spiritually, it might signify the presence of a powerful protective energy, the process of purification, or the connection to deep, transformative forces.

Ocean

The ocean in dreams often symbolizes the subconscious mind, emotions, or the vastness of life. **Swimming in the ocean** might suggest exploring deep emotions or facing life's challenges, while **drowning in the ocean** could indicate feeling overwhelmed or lost. Psychologically, the ocean can represent the mind's exploration of its depths or the presence of powerful emotions. Spiritually, it might signify the flow of life, the presence of divine mystery, or the connection to the collective unconscious.

Oasis

An oasis in dreams often symbolizes relief, refuge, or a source of nourishment. **Finding an oasis** might suggest discovering a source of comfort or relief in a challenging situation, while **missing an oasis** could indicate feelings of despair or fear of losing something valuable. Psychologically, an oasis can represent the mind's focus on finding peace, sustenance, or hope in difficult times. Spiritually, it might signify a sacred space, the presence of divine sustenance, or the fulfilment of a deep longing.

Office

Offices in dreams often symbolize work, responsibility, or the pursuit of goals. **Being in an office** might suggest the need to focus on your responsibilities or pursue professional goals, while **seeing an office in disarray** could indicate feelings of disorganization or stress related to work. Psychologically, offices represent the mind's focus on work, responsibility, and goals. Spiritually, they may signify divine guidance in professional pursuits, the resolution of spiritual responsibilities, or the pursuit of sacred goals.

Orange

Orange in dreams often symbolizes enthusiasm, creativity, and social interactions. Dreaming of orange might reflect a desire for excitement or a need to express yourself more creatively. Psychologically, it represents the focus on vibrant energy and social connections. Spiritually, it may signify divine encouragement to embrace your creative and social potential.

Olive

Olive, a muted green-brown, often symbolizes peace, compromise, and healing. Seeing olive might suggest the need for reconciliation or indicate that healing is taking place. Psychologically, it represents a focus on finding balance and resolving conflicts. Spiritually, it may signify divine support in achieving peace and understanding.

Orchard

Orchards in dreams often symbolize abundance, growth, or the fruits of one's labour. **Walking through an orchard** might suggest enjoying the rewards of your efforts or a period of prosperity, while **a barren orchard** could indicate missed opportunities or lack of growth. Psychologically, orchards can represent the mind's focus on productivity, creativity, or the results of hard work. Spiritually, they might signify the harvest of spiritual wisdom, the nurturing of the soul, or the presence of divine abundance.

Opera

Operas in dreams often symbolize drama, expression, or the performance of emotions. **Attending an opera** might suggest the need to express your emotions or the presence of dramatic situations in your life, while **performing in an opera** could indicate the desire to showcase your talents or emotions. Psychologically, operas represent the mind's focus on drama, expression, and performance. Spiritually, they may signify the manifestation of divine expression, the pursuit of spiritual performance, or the exploration of sacred emotions.

Orientation

Dreams about orientation often symbolize the need to find your direction or adjust to new situations. Attending an orientation in a dream might reflect the process of adjusting to new circumstances or seeking guidance. Psychologically, it represents the focus on finding direction or adapting to changes. Spiritually, it may signify divine guidance in navigating new paths or understanding your purpose.

Oxygen

Oxygen in dreams often symbolizes life, breath, or the need for renewal. Oxygen being the focus of your dream might suggest the need for renewal or the presence of life-giving energy, while **experiencing difficulty breathing** could indicate feelings of suffocation or the need for spiritual renewal. Psychologically, oxygen represents the mind's focus on life, breath, and renewal. Spiritually, it may signify divine breath, the pursuit of spiritual renewal, or the presence of sacred life-giving energy.

Owl

Owls in dreams often symbolize wisdom, intuition, or the ability to see beyond the surface. **Seeing an owl** might suggest gaining insight or understanding something previously unknown, while **being attacked by an owl** could indicate fear of the truth or a challenge to one's wisdom. Psychologically, owls can represent the mind's focus on knowledge, perception, or the ability to see beyond the surface. Spiritually, they might signify a connection to higher wisdom, the presence of a spirit guide, or the unveiling of hidden truths.

P

Paths

Paths in dreams often represent life direction, choices, or the journey of the soul. **A clear path** might suggest confidence or a sense of purpose, while **a blocked or confusing path** could indicate uncertainty or obstacles in waking life. Psychologically, paths can symbolize the direction of one's thoughts or life decisions. Spiritually, they may signify the journey towards enlightenment or one's spiritual path.

People

Dreams involving people often symbolize aspects of the dreamer's personality or relationships. **Seeing a familiar person** might reflect the dreamer's feelings or unresolved issues with that person, while **seeing a stranger** could indicate unknown aspects of oneself. Psychologically, people in dreams can represent different parts of the psyche. Spiritually, they might symbolize guides, teachers, or soul connections.

Phone

Phones in dreams often symbolize communication, connection, or the need to reach out. **Using a phone** might suggest the need to communicate or connect with others, while **having difficulty using a phone** could indicate challenges in communication or connection. Psychologically, phones represent the mind's focus on communication, connection, and reaching out. Spiritually, they may signify divine communication, the pursuit of spiritual connection, or the resolution of sacred communication issues.

Plant

Plants in dreams often symbolize growth, potential, or the need for nurturing. **Seeing a healthy plant** might suggest the presence of potential or the need for growth, while **seeing a wilting plant** could indicate feelings of stagnation or neglect. Psychologically, plants represent the mind's focus on growth, potential, and nurturing. Spiritually, they may signify divine growth, the manifestation of spiritual potential, or the nurturing of sacred aspects of the soul.

Pregnancy

Pregnancy in dreams often symbolizes creation, growth, or the potential for new beginnings. Being pregnant might suggest the development of a new idea, project, or phase of life. Psychologically, pregnancy can reflect a desire for change, creativity, or nurturing. Spiritually, it may symbolize the birth of new spiritual insights or the growth of inner wisdom.

Promotion

Dreams about promotion often symbolize achievement, recognition, or career advancement. **Receiving a promotion** in a dream might reflect feelings of accomplishment or the desire for career growth, while **missing out on a promotion** could indicate concerns about recognition or progress. Psychologically, it represents the focus on success and advancement. Spiritually, it may signify divine affirmation of your efforts or guidance towards higher goals.

Purple

Purple in dreams often symbolizes spirituality, creativity, and royalty. Seeing purple might suggest a focus on spiritual matters or indicate creative inspiration. Psychologically, it represents the pursuit of higher ideals and self-expression. Spiritually, it may signify divine guidance and support in your spiritual and creative endeavors.

Pyramid

Pyramids in dreams often symbolize ancient wisdom, mystery, or spiritual ascent. **Climbing a pyramid** might suggest the pursuit of knowledge or spiritual enlightenment, while **seeing a pyramid** could indicate the presence of ancient or hidden knowledge. Psychologically, pyramids can represent the mind's focus on structure, stability, or reaching a higher state of consciousness. Spiritually, they might signify the connection to divine energies, the journey to higher realms, or the alignment of mind, body, and spirit.

Portal

Portals in dreams often symbolize gateways to new experiences, transformations, or different dimensions. **Entering a portal** might suggest the beginning of a new phase in life or a shift in consciousness, while **being afraid to enter a portal** could indicate fear of the unknown or resistance to change. Psychologically, portals can represent the mind's readiness to embrace change or explore new possibilities. Spiritually, they might signify the crossing of thresholds, the journey into the unknown, or the transition between worlds.

Puppy

Puppies in dreams often symbolize innocence, loyalty, or new beginnings. **Playing with a puppy** might suggest a need for affection or the desire to nurture something, while seeing **a lost puppy** could indicate feelings of abandonment or a need for guidance. Psychologically, puppies can represent the mind's focus on companionship, playfulness, or the nurturing aspect of oneself. Spiritually, they might signify unconditional love, the presence of a spirit guide, or the purity of the soul.

Queen

Queens in dreams often symbolize authority, power, or the feminine aspect of leadership. **Seeing a queen** might suggest the presence of feminine authority or the need to embrace leadership roles, while **being dethroned** could indicate feelings of diminished power or loss of control. Psychologically, queens represent the mind's focus on authority, power, and leadership. Spiritually, they may signify divine feminine authority, the manifestation of spiritual power, or the need to embrace spiritual leadership.

Quest

Quests in dreams often symbolize journeys, goals, or the pursuit of deeper understanding. **Embarking on a quest** might suggest the pursuit of personal or spiritual goals or the journey of self-discovery, while **failing a quest** could indicate challenges or obstacles in achieving your aspirations. Psychologically, quests represent the mind's focus on journeys, goals, and understanding. Spiritually, they may signify the pursuit of divine goals, the journey of the soul, or the exploration of sacred truths.

Question

Questions in dreams often symbolize the search for answers, curiosity, or uncertainty. **Asking a question** might suggest the need to seek answers or address uncertainties, while **being asked a question** could indicate the presence of curiosity or the need to address specific issues. Psychologically, questions represent the mind's focus on answers, curiosity, and uncertainty. Spiritually, they may signify divine inquiry, the pursuit of spiritual answers, or the exploration of sacred uncertainties.

Quicksand

Quicksand in dreams often symbolizes feelings of being trapped, overwhelmed, or stuck in a situation. **Sinking in quicksand** might suggest anxiety or fears of losing control, while **escaping quicksand** could indicate overcoming obstacles or fears. Psychologically, quicksand can represent the mind's response to situations that seem to pull one down or the fear of losing control. Spiritually, it might signify the challenges of navigating life's uncertainties, the need for grounding, or the struggle against inner turmoil.

Quilt

Quilts in dreams often symbolize warmth, protection, or the patchwork of life's experiences. **Being wrapped in a quilt** might suggest comfort or the desire for security, while seeing **a torn quilt** could indicate feelings of vulnerability or loss. Psychologically, quilts can represent the mind's focus on preserving memories, traditions, or the need for emotional warmth. Spiritually, they might signify the weaving together of life's lessons, the protection of ancestral wisdom, or the comfort of spiritual guidance.

Qualification

Dreams about qualifications often symbolize competence, achievement, or the need to prove yourself. **Achieving a qualification** in a dream might reflect a sense of accomplishment or readiness for new challenges, while **failing to qualify** could indicate feelings of inadequacy or the need for further development. Psychologically, it represents concerns about performance and self-worth. Spiritually, it may signify divine approval or the need for further growth.

Quitting

Dreams about quitting often symbolize the need to let go, make changes, or address dissatisfaction. Quitting a job or relationship in a dream might reflect a desire for change or the need to release something that no longer serves you. Psychologically, it represents feelings of dissatisfaction or the need for new direction. Spiritually, it may signify the need for divine guidance in letting go or pursuing new paths.

Quiet

Quiet in dreams often symbolizes peace, solitude, or introspection. **A quiet environment** might suggest a need for inner calm or reflection, while an **unnerving quiet** could indicate feelings of isolation or fear of the unknown. Psychologically, quiet can represent mental clarity or the suppression of thoughts. Spiritually, it might signify the stillness needed to connect with higher consciousness or the divine.

Quarrel

Quarrels in dreams often symbolize inner conflict, unresolved issues, or tension with others. **Arguing with someone** might suggest feelings of frustration or the need to express oneself, while **witnessing a quarrel** could indicate anxiety about conflict or a desire to avoid confrontation. Psychologically, quarrels can represent the mind's attempt to process disagreements, anger, or stress. Spiritually, they might signify the struggle between opposing forces, the need for harmony, or the resolution of karmic debts.

R

Rain

Rain in dreams often symbolizes cleansing, renewal, or emotional release. **Walking in the rain** might suggest a desire to cleanse oneself of negative emotions or the need for emotional healing, while **a stormy rain** could indicate overwhelming emotions or a turbulent situation. Psychologically, rain can represent the mind's process of washing away old thoughts or feelings. Spiritually, it might signify the blessing of renewal, the nurturing of the soul, or the presence of divine grace.

Rainbow

Rainbows in dreams often symbolize hope, promise, or the connection between the physical and spiritual realms. **Seeing a rainbow** might suggest the arrival of good fortune or the fulfilment of a dream, while **chasing a rainbow** could indicate the pursuit of an elusive goal. Psychologically, rainbows can represent the mind's focus on optimism, harmony, or the integration of different aspects of life. Spiritually, they might signify the presence of divine blessing, the bridge between worlds, or the realization of inner peace.

Red

Red in dreams often symbolizes passion, energy, and action. Dreaming of red might reflect strong emotions or a need to assert yourself. Psychologically, it represents the focus on drive and vitality. Spiritually, it may signify divine encouragement to embrace your passions and pursue your goals with enthusiasm.

Retirement

Dreams about retirement often symbolize the completion of a significant phase, relaxation, or the need to evaluate your life's direction. Retiring from a job in a dream might reflect a sense of accomplishment or the need for rest and reflection. Psychologically, it represents the focus on transitioning to a new phase of life. Spiritually, it may signify divine guidance in finding new purpose or enjoying the fruits of your labor.

Reunion

Dreams about reunions often symbolize reconnection, reconciliation, or the desire to address past relationships. Reuniting with someone in a dream might reflect a desire for closure or the need to resolve past issues. Psychologically, it represents the focus on reconciling with others or finding closure. Spiritually, it may signify divine healing and the importance of reconnection.

Ring

Rings in dreams often symbolize commitment, unity, or eternity. **Wearing a ring** might suggest a commitment to a relationship or a personal vow, while **losing a ring** could indicate fear of losing a connection or breaking a promise. Psychologically, rings can represent the mind's focus on relationships, promises, or the desire for completeness. Spiritually, they might signify the unbroken circle of life, the connection between the physical and spiritual, or the eternal bond of love.

River

Rivers in dreams often symbolize the flow of life, emotions, or the journey of the soul. **Flowing with a river** might suggest going with the flow of life or the passage of time, while **struggling against the current** could indicate resistance to change or emotional turmoil. Psychologically, rivers can represent the mind's exploration of emotions, the passage through life's stages, or the process of letting go. Spiritually, they might signify the flow of divine energy, the journey toward spiritual awakening, or the connection to the source of life.

Rope

Ropes in dreams often symbolize connections, constraints, or the need to hold on. **Seeing a rope** might suggest the need to connect with others or the presence of constraints, while **being tied with a rope** could indicate feelings of restriction or the need to hold on to something. Psychologically, ropes represent the mind's focus on connections, constraints, and holding on. Spiritually, they may signify divine connections, the resolution of spiritual constraints, or the need for sacred support.

Rose

Rose, a soft pink, often symbolizes romance, gentleness, and appreciation. Dreaming of rose might reflect desires for love or indicate feelings of tenderness and affection. Psychologically, it represents the focus on romantic or emotional fulfillment. Spiritually, it may signify divine blessings in matters of the heart and personal connections.

Rose Quartz (Crystal/Mineral)

Rose quartz represents love, compassion, and emotional healing. Dreaming of rose quartz might suggest that you are focusing on self-love, nurturing relationships, or healing emotional wounds. It can also indicate a need to open your heart and embrace love and compassion in your life.

Roses

Roses in dreams often symbolize love, beauty, or the unfolding of spiritual truth. **Receiving a rose** might suggest love or appreciation from others, while seeing **a withered rose** could indicate lost love or the passing of beauty. Psychologically, roses can represent the mind's focus on affection, the appreciation of beauty, or the experience of loss. Spiritually, they might signify the unfolding of the soul, the presence of divine love, or the path to enlightenment.

S

Scarlet

Scarlet, a bright red, often symbolizes intense emotion, urgency, and vitality. Dreaming of scarlet might reflect strong feelings or a need for immediate action. Psychologically, it represents the focus on high energy and urgent matters. Spiritually, it may signify divine encouragement to address passionate pursuits or urgent issues.

Ship

Ships in dreams often symbolize journeys, exploration, or the passage through different phases of life. **Seeing a ship** might suggest the need for exploration or the presence of a journey, while seeing **a ship in distress** could indicate challenges or obstacles in navigating through different phases of your life. Psychologically, ships represent the mind's focus on journeys, exploration, and life phases. Spiritually, they may signify divine guidance in your journey, the exploration of spiritual realms, or the resolution of sacred challenges.

Silver

Silver in dreams often symbolizes intuition, reflection, and transformation. Seeing silver might suggest a need for introspection or indicate that change is occurring. Psychologically, it represents the focus on inner reflection and adaptability. Spiritually, it may signify divine guidance and support in navigating transformations and gaining insights.

Snake

Snakes in dreams often symbolize transformation, hidden fears, or the need to confront deep-seated issues. **Seeing a snake** might suggest the presence of hidden fears or the need for transformation, while **being bitten by a snake** could indicate the need to address deep-seated issues or confront personal fears. Psychologically, snakes represent the mind's focus on transformation, fears, and hidden issues. Spiritually, they may signify divine transformation, the resolution of spiritual fears, or the pursuit of sacred healing.

Snow

Snow symbolizes purity, stillness, and sometimes emotional coldness. In dreams, snow can indicate a need for rest, reflection, or a break from emotional intensity. It may also suggest a period of tranquility or the need to address feelings of emotional distance.

Spider

Spiders in dreams often symbolize creativity, patience, or the weaving of one's life path. **Seeing a spider** might suggest the presence of creativity or the need to address complex situations, while **seeing a spider's web** could indicate the weaving of your life path or the presence of intricate connections. Psychologically, spiders represent the mind's focus on creativity, patience, and complex situations. Spiritually, they may signify divine creativity, the weaving of spiritual paths, or the exploration of sacred connections.

Stairs

Stairs in dreams often symbolize progress, ascent, or the journey to higher levels of understanding. **Climbing stairs** might suggest the pursuit of personal or spiritual goals or the progression to higher levels of understanding, while **seeing broken stairs** could indicate obstacles or challenges in making progress. Psychologically, stairs represent the mind's focus on progress, ascent, and understanding. Spiritually, they may signify the elevation of the soul, the pursuit of divine goals, or the overcoming of sacred challenges.

Star

Stars in dreams often symbolize hope, guidance, or the connection to the divine. **Seeing a bright star** might suggest the presence of a guiding force or the fulfilment of a wish, while **following a star** could indicate the pursuit of a goal or spiritual journey. Psychologically, stars can represent the mind's focus on aspirations, inspiration, or the presence of hope. Spiritually, they might signify the connection to higher realms, the presence of divine guidance, or the illumination of the path ahead.

Storm

Storms in dreams often symbolize turmoil, chaos, or emotional upheaval. **Being caught in a storm** might suggest feeling overwhelmed by emotions or facing a challenging situation, while **seeing a storm pass** could indicate the resolution of conflict or the return of peace. Psychologically, storms can represent the mind's response to stress, anger, or inner conflict. Spiritually, they might signify the presence of powerful transformative forces, the purging of negativity, or the renewal of the soul.

Sunshine

Sunshine in dreams is linked to happiness, energy, and success. It reflects a positive outlook, vitality, and divine favour. Dreaming of sunshine suggests that you are experiencing or anticipating a period of joy, achievement, and overall well-being.

Swimming

Swimming in dreams often represents navigating emotions, exploring the unconscious, or the ability to stay afloat amidst life's challenges. **Swimming in calm waters** might suggest emotional balance or clarity, while **struggling in turbulent waters** could indicate emotional overwhelm or inner conflict. Psychologically, swimming can symbolize one's ability to cope with or adapt to circumstances. Spiritually, it might signify immersion in one's emotional or spiritual life.

T

Teal

Teal, a deep blue-green, often symbolizes emotional depth, balance, and sophistication. Seeing teal might suggest a need for emotional balance or indicate that you are dealing with complex emotions. Psychologically, it represents the focus on emotional intelligence and stability. Spiritually, it may signify divine guidance in achieving balance and understanding.

Teeth

Teeth in dreams often symbolize personal power, confidence, or communication. **Losing teeth** might suggest feelings of vulnerability, loss of control, or anxieties about aging or appearance, while **having strong teeth** could indicate confidence or vitality. Psychologically, teeth can represent anxieties about self-image or fears of inadequacy. Spiritually, losing teeth may signify a shedding of old beliefs or a need for renewal.

Temple

Temples in dreams often symbolize spirituality, reverence, or the pursuit of sacred goals. **Seeing a temple** might suggest the presence of spiritual aspirations or the need to pursue sacred goals, while **seeing a temple in disrepair** could indicate feelings of disconnection or challenges in your spiritual journey. Psychologically, temples represent the mind's focus on spirituality, reverence, and sacred goals. Spiritually, they may signify divine guidance, the pursuit of spiritual aspirations, or the resolution of sacred challenges.

Termination

Dreams about termination often symbolize the end of a phase, job, or relationship. Experiencing a termination in a dream might reflect feelings of loss or the need to address the end of a significant aspect of your life. Psychologically, it represents the focus on dealing with endings and transitions. Spiritually, it may signify the need for divine support in navigating closures or finding new beginnings.

Thorns

Thorns in dreams often symbolize pain, obstacles, or protection. **Being pricked by thorns** might suggest encountering difficulties or feeling hurt, while **seeing a thorny bush** could indicate the presence of challenges or the need for caution. Psychologically, thorns can represent the mind's focus on pain, defense mechanisms, or the barriers to growth. Spiritually, they might signify the presence of trials, the protection of something sacred, or the purification through suffering.

Thunder

Thunder in dreams often symbolizes powerful emotions, anger, or a sudden realization. **Hearing thunder** might suggest an impending emotional storm or a warning, while **seeing lightning with thunder** could indicate a flash of insight or sudden clarity. Psychologically, thunder can represent repressed anger or a buildup of tension that needs release. Spiritually, it may symbolize divine messages, the voice of the gods, or the power of nature.

Tiger

Tigers in dreams often symbolize power, strength, or the need to confront inner fears. **Seeing a tiger** might suggest the presence of powerful energies or the need to confront inner fears, while **being chased by a tiger** could indicate the need to address feelings of vulnerability or the presence of intense emotions. Psychologically, tigers represent the mind's focus on power, strength, and fears. Spiritually, they may signify divine strength, the resolution of spiritual fears, or the exploration of sacred power.

Tiger's Eye (Crystal/Mineral)

Tiger's eye symbolizes courage, strength, and grounding. Seeing tiger's eye in a dream can indicate that you are drawing on your inner strength and resilience. It may also suggest that you need to stay grounded and focused as you face challenges or make important decisions.

Train

Trains in dreams often symbolize progress, direction, or the journey of life. **Seeing a train** might suggest the need for progress or direction in your life, while **missing a train** could indicate feelings of missed opportunities or delays. Psychologically, trains represent the mind's focus on progress, direction, and the journey. Spiritually, they may signify divine guidance, the pursuit of spiritual direction, or the resolution of sacred delays

Travel

Dreams about travel often symbolize exploration, change, or the journey of life. **Traveling to a new destination** in a dream might reflect a desire for adventure or new experiences, while **getting lost while traveling** could indicate uncertainties or challenges. Psychologically, it represents the process of exploring new opportunities or changes. Spiritually, it may signify divine guidance in navigating life's journey or pursuing spiritual quests.

Tree

Trees in dreams often symbolize growth, stability, or the connection between heaven and earth. **Climbing a tree** might suggest personal growth or reaching for higher knowledge, while **seeing a tree with deep roots** could indicate stability or a strong foundation. Psychologically, trees can represent the mind's focus on development, grounding, or the integration of different aspects of the self. Spiritually, they might signify the connection to the earth, the axis mundi (world tree), or the presence of ancestral wisdom.

Tornado

Tornadoes in dreams often symbolize chaos, upheaval, or the

need to address significant changes. Seeing a tornado might suggest the presence of chaos or upheaval in your life, while being caught in a tornado could indicate feelings of being overwhelmed or the need to address significant changes. Psychologically, tornadoes represent the mind's focus on chaos, upheaval, and change. Spiritually, they may signify divine upheaval, the resolution of sacred chaos, or the exploration of significant spiritual changes.

Tsunami

Tsunamis in dreams often symbolize overwhelming emotions, sudden change, or the fear of being overwhelmed. **Being caught in a tsunami** might suggest feeling powerless in the face of strong emotions or external forces, while **watching a tsunami from afar** could indicate awareness of impending change or the anticipation of emotional upheaval. Psychologically, tsunamis can represent the mind's response to repressed emotions, fears, or the impact of significant life events. Spiritually, they might signify the presence of powerful transformative energies, the cleansing of the old, or the awakening of deep emotional truths.

Tunnel

Tunnels in dreams often symbolize transition, exploration, or the journey to the subconscious. **Walking through a tunnel** might suggest going through a difficult period or exploring hidden aspects of oneself, while **seeing the end of a tunnel** could indicate the approach of clarity or resolution. Psychologically, tunnels can represent the mind's process of moving through challenges, the exploration of inner depths, or the transition between phases of life. Spiritually, they might signify the journey through the shadow, the passage to a new phase, or the connection to hidden realms.

Turquoise

Turquoise, a blue-green, often symbolizes tranquillity, communication, and healing. Dreaming of turquoise might indicate a need for calm communication or suggest that healing is occurring. Psychologically, it represents the desire for peace and clear expression. Spiritually, it may signify divine support in achieving harmony and healing.

U

UFO

UFOs in dreams often symbolize the unknown, curiosity, or the presence of unexplained phenomena. **Seeing a UFO** might suggest the presence of curiosity or the need to explore the unknown, while **witnessing a UFO land** could indicate the revelation of new insights or the presence of unexplained phenomena in your life. Psychologically, UFOs represent the mind's focus on the unknown, curiosity, and unexplained phenomena. Spiritually, they may signify divine revelations, the exploration of sacred mysteries, or the pursuit of spiritual insights.

Umbrella

Umbrellas in dreams often symbolize protection, shelter, or the ability to navigate emotional storms. **Holding an umbrella** might suggest readiness to face emotional storms or protect oneself from outside influences, while **losing an umbrella** could indicate vulnerability or lack of preparation. Psychologically, umbrellas can represent one's defence mechanisms or emotional boundaries. Spiritually, they may signify divine protection or a reminder to stay sheltered in one's faith during difficult times.

Underwater

Being underwater in dreams often symbolizes deep emotions, the subconscious mind, or the exploration of hidden aspects of oneself. **Swimming underwater** might suggest diving into deep emotions or exploring the subconscious, while **struggling to breathe underwater** could indicate feelings of being overwhelmed or suffocated by emotions. Psychologically, being underwater can represent the mind's process of confronting hidden fears, desires, or unresolved issues. Spiritually, it might signify the journey into the depths of the soul, the connection to the collective unconscious, or the exploration of spiritual mysteries.

Unemployment

Dreams about unemployment often symbolize feelings of inadequacy, change, or the need to address personal goals. Experiencing unemployment in a dream might reflect concerns about career direction or self-worth. Psychologically, it represents the focus on job satisfaction and personal fulfillment. Spiritually, it may signify the need for divine guidance in finding purpose or pursuing new opportunities.

Unexpected Event

Dreams about unexpected events often symbolize unpredictability, stress, or the need to adapt to changes. Encountering an unexpected event in a dream might reflect anxieties about unforeseen circumstances or the need to be flexible. Psychologically, it represents the focus on managing uncertainty or stress. Spiritually, it may signify divine assistance in navigating surprises or finding clarity amidst chaos.

Unicorn

Unicorns in dreams often symbolize purity, magic, or the presence of something rare and special. **Seeing a unicorn** might suggest the discovery of something precious or the presence of hope, while **riding a unicorn** could indicate a journey toward spiritual fulfilment or the pursuit of a dream. Psychologically, unicorns can represent the mind's focus on idealism, the pursuit of perfection, or the belief in the extraordinary. Spiritually, they might signify the embodiment of divine purity, the presence of magical forces, or the realization of one's highest potential.

Uniform

Uniforms in dreams often symbolize conformity, roles, or the need to fit in. **Seeing a uniform** might suggest the need to conform to specific roles or expectations, while **wearing a uniform** could indicate the desire to fit in or the presence of specific responsibilities. Psychologically, uniforms represent the mind's focus on conformity, roles, and fitting in. Spiritually, they may signify divine roles, the exploration of sacred responsibilities, or the pursuit of spiritual conformity.

Urn

Urns in dreams often symbolize the containment of memories, the past, or the presence of something sacred. **Seeing an urn** might suggest reflecting on past experiences or the desire to preserve something valuable, while **breaking an urn** could indicate the release of repressed emotions or the fear of losing something important. Psychologically, urns can represent the mind's focus on memory, loss, or the containment of powerful emotions. Spiritually, they might signify the vessel of the soul, the preservation of spiritual wisdom, or the connection to ancestors.

V

Vanilla

Vanilla, a soft off-white, often symbolizes simplicity, comfort, and subtlety. Seeing vanilla might suggest a focus on ease and comfort in your life. Psychologically, it represents the desire for simplicity and gentle experiences. Spiritually, it may signify divine encouragement to appreciate the simple pleasures and find comfort in subtlety.

Vampire

Vampires in dreams often symbolize draining relationships, fear of death, or hidden desires. **Being attacked by a vampire** might suggest feeling drained by someone or something in your life, while **becoming a vampire** could indicate a fear of one's own dark desires or the temptation to exploit others. Psychologically, vampires can represent the mind's focus on parasitic relationships, repressed desires, or the fear of mortality. Spiritually, they might signify the struggle between the physical and spiritual, the presence of dark energies, or the challenge of overcoming base instincts.

Vehicles

Vehicles in dreams often symbolize one's journey, direction, or the means to achieve goals. **Driving a vehicle** might suggest control over one's life path, while **being a passenger** could indicate dependency or lack of control. A broken vehicle might reflect obstacles or setbacks. Psychologically, vehicles can represent one's drive, ambition, or state of mind. Spiritually, they may symbolize the journey of the soul or the pursuit of spiritual objectives.

Vineyard

Vineyards in dreams often symbolize abundance, growth, or the fruits of one's labour. **Walking through a vineyard** might suggest enjoying the rewards of your efforts or a period of productivity, while **seeing a barren vineyard** could indicate missed opportunities or lack of growth. Psychologically, vineyards can represent the mind's focus on creativity, fertility, or the results of hard work. Spiritually, they might signify the harvest of spiritual wisdom, the nurturing of the soul, or the presence of divine abundance.

Violet

Violet in dreams often symbolizes spirituality, creativity, and transformation. Dreaming of violet might reflect spiritual insights or indicate a focus on creative projects. Psychologically, it represents the pursuit of higher consciousness and self-expression. Spiritually, it may signify divine inspiration and support in your spiritual and creative growth.

Voices

Hearing voices in dreams often symbolizes guidance, intuition, or unresolved thoughts. **A comforting voice** might suggest reassurance or inner wisdom, while **a frightening voice** could indicate fear, guilt, or negative self-talk. Psychologically, voices can represent internal conflicts or the influence of others' opinions. Spiritually, they may signify messages from spirit guides, angels, or the higher self.

Volcano

Volcanoes in dreams often symbolize repressed emotions, potential outbursts, or a powerful transformation. **An erupting volcano** might suggest pent-up anger, passion, or a situation that is about to explode, while **a dormant volcano** could indicate underlying tension or potential. Psychologically, volcanoes can represent emotional release or the pressure of unresolved issues. Spiritually, they may signify a profound awakening, a release of spiritual energy, or a transformative event.

Vulture

Vultures in dreams often symbolize death, decay, or the process of purification. **Seeing a vulture** might suggest the presence of something that needs to be let go of or the anticipation of an ending, while **being attacked by a vulture** could indicate fear of loss or the presence of a threatening situation. Psychologically, vultures can represent the mind's focus on death, transformation, or the need to cleanse oneself of negative influences. Spiritually, they might signify the presence of powerful purifying energies, the cycle of life and death, or the process of letting go.

W

Wagon

Wagons in dreams often symbolize movement, progress, or the journey of life. **Seeing a wagon** might suggest the presence of movement or progress in your life, while **seeing a wagon stuck or broken down** could indicate obstacles or delays in your journey. Psychologically, wagons represent the mind's focus on movement, progress, and life's journey. Spiritually, they may signify divine movement, the pursuit of spiritual progress, or the resolution of sacred delays.

Waterfall

Waterfalls in dreams often symbolize the release of emotions, the flow of energy, or the presence of significant change. **Seeing a waterfall** might suggest the need for emotional release or the presence of powerful energy, while **seeing a waterfall that is blocked** could indicate obstacles in your emotional flow or the need for change. Psychologically, waterfalls represent the mind's focus on emotional release, energy flow, and change. Spiritually, they may signify divine release, the pursuit of spiritual flow, or the resolution of sacred obstacles.

Wedding

Dreams about weddings often symbolize commitment, union, or the merging of different aspects of your life. **Attending a wedding** might reflect a focus on relationships or personal unions, while **planning or participating in a wedding** could indicate a desire for commitment or integration. Psychologically, it represents the focus on connection and unity. Spiritually, it may signify divine affirmation or the alignment of personal and spiritual goals.

White

White in dreams often symbolizes purity, innocence, and new beginnings. Dreaming of white might indicate a fresh start or a focus on purity and clarity. Psychologically, it represents the desire for a clean slate and personal integrity. Spiritually, it may signify divine blessings and guidance in starting anew or seeking spiritual purity.

Wind

Wind denotes change, freedom, or external influences. Dreaming of wind suggests that you need to adapt to shifting circumstances or that external forces are affecting your situation. It can also symbolize a desire for freedom or the movement of ideas and emotions.

Window

Windows in dreams often symbolize opportunities, perspectives, or the need to see things clearly. **Seeing a window** might suggest the presence of opportunities or the need to gain a new perspective, while seeing **a window that is closed or dirty** could indicate obstacles or difficulties in seeing things clearly. Psychologically, windows represent the mind's focus on opportunities, perspectives, and clarity. Spiritually, they may signify divine opportunities, the pursuit of spiritual clarity, or the exploration of sacred perspectives.

Wine

Wine, a deep red, often symbolizes richness, pleasure, and reflection. Seeing wine might reflect indulgence or a focus on enjoying life's pleasures. Psychologically, it represents the pursuit of enjoyment and reflection. Spiritually, it may signify divine encouragement to embrace life's richness and savor meaningful experiences.

Wings

Wings in dreams often symbolize freedom, transcendence, or the desire to rise above challenges. **Having wings** might suggest the desire for freedom or the ability to overcome obstacles, while **seeing an angel's wings** could indicate the presence of divine protection or guidance. Psychologically, wings can represent the mind's focus on escape, aspiration, or the longing for freedom. Spiritually, they might signify the presence of divine beings, the journey of the soul, or the elevation of consciousness.

Witch

Witches in dreams often symbolize transformation, hidden powers, or the presence of mystical forces. **Seeing a witch** might suggest the presence of transformation or the need to address hidden powers, while **being confronted by a witch** could indicate the need to confront mystical or spiritual challenges. Psychologically, witches represent the mind's focus on transformation, hidden powers, and mystical forces. Spiritually, they may signify divine transformation, the exploration of spiritual powers, or the resolution of sacred challenges.

Wolf

Wolves in dreams often symbolize instinct, independence, or the need to confront personal fears. **Seeing a wolf** might suggest the presence of powerful instincts or the need to address personal fears, while **being chased by a wolf** could indicate the need to confront or address deep-seated anxieties. Psychologically, wolves represent the mind's focus on instincts, independence, and fears. Spiritually, they may signify divine instincts, the resolution of spiritual fears, or the exploration of sacred independence.

Worm

Worms in dreams often symbolize decay, renewal, or the presence of something hidden. **Seeing a worm** might suggest feelings of disgust or the awareness of something decaying, while **being surrounded by worms** could indicate fear of corruption or the presence of repressed emotions. Psychologically, worms can represent the mind's focus on decay, the process of renewal, or the confrontation of something unpleasant. Spiritually, they might signify the process of transformation, the cycle of life and death, or the presence of hidden forces.

Wound

Wounds in dreams often symbolize pain, healing, or vulnerability. **Having a wound** might suggest feelings of hurt or the need for healing, while **seeing someone else's wound** could indicate empathy or awareness of others' pain. Psychologically, wounds can represent the mind's focus on unresolved trauma, the process of healing, or the acknowledgment of vulnerability. Spiritually, they might signify the presence of karmic wounds, the opportunity for spiritual growth, or the embodiment of the wounded healer archetype.

X-Ray

X-rays in dreams often symbolize the need to look deeper, uncover hidden truths, or examine oneself more closely. **Having an X-ray** might suggest concerns about health or fears of being exposed, while **seeing through someone with an X-ray** could indicate a desire to see through deception or to understand someone better. Psychologically, X-rays can represent a need for self-examination or transparency. Spiritually, they may signify the ability to see beyond the surface or to perceive spiritual truths.

Xenophobia

Dreams about xenophobia often symbolize fears of the unknown, otherness, or cultural differences. Experiencing xenophobia in a dream might reflect anxieties about unfamiliar situations or people. Psychologically, it represents concerns about integrating with different cultures or facing new experiences. Spiritually, it may signify the need for divine guidance in overcoming fears and embracing diversity.

Xylophone

A xylophone in a dream often symbolizes harmony, rhythm, or communication. **Playing a xylophone** might suggest a desire to create harmony in one's life or to express oneself creatively, while **hearing a xylophone** could indicate a call to pay attention to the 'music' or rhythms of life. Psychologically, it can represent childhood, playfulness, or the desire for simplicity. Spiritually, it may symbolize becoming attuned to higher vibrations or the music of the spheres.

Yacht

A yacht in a dream often symbolizes luxury, relaxation, or a journey of leisure. **Sailing on a yacht** might suggest freedom, adventure, or the pursuit of pleasure, while **a yacht in rough seas** could indicate challenges in a seemingly secure or pleasurable situation. Psychologically, yachts can represent the desire for status, wealth, or comfort. Spiritually, they may symbolize a spiritual journey taken in comfort or the exploration of the soul's vast oceans.

Yarn

Yarn in dreams often symbolizes creativity, connection, or the weaving of life's experiences. **Knitting with yarn** might suggest the desire to create something meaningful or to connect different aspects of life, while **seeing tangled yarn** could indicate feelings of confusion or the need to untangle a situation. Psychologically, yarn can represent the mind's focus on creativity, the process of weaving life's experiences together, or the desire for connection. Spiritually, it might signify the thread of life, the connection to the divine, or the weaving of destiny.

Yawn

Yawning in dreams often symbolizes tiredness, boredom, or the need for relaxation. **Yawning yourself** might suggest feelings of fatigue or the need to take a break, while **seeing someone else yawn** could indicate empathy or awareness of others' emotions. Psychologically, yawns can represent the mind's focus on relaxation, the need to release tension, or the acknowledgment of boredom. Spiritually, they might signify the release of stagnant energy, the need for rest, or the indication of a shift in consciousness.

Yearning

Dreams about yearning often symbolize desires, unfulfilled needs, or the search for meaning. Yearning for something in a dream might reflect deep-seated desires or the need to address unmet needs. Psychologically, it represents the focus on desires or the search for fulfillment. Spiritually, it may signify divine guidance in pursuing deeper meaning or addressing inner longings.

Yelling

Yelling in dreams often symbolizes frustration, anger, or the need to express oneself. **Yelling at someone** might suggest unresolved conflict or the need to communicate more effectively, while **being yelled at** could indicate feelings of guilt, anxiety, or oppression. Psychologically, yelling can represent a release of pent-up emotions or a cry for attention. Spiritually, it may signify a need to voice one's truth or to call out for spiritual guidance.

Yellow

Yellow in dreams often symbolizes happiness, optimism, or the presence of intellectual energy. **Seeing something yellow** might suggest the presence of joy or the awakening of intellectual pursuits, while **wearing yellow** could indicate a desire to stand out or to embrace positivity. Psychologically, yellow can represent the mind's focus on optimism, clarity, or the stimulation of mental energy. Spiritually, it might signify the presence of divine light, the activation of the solar plexus chakra, or the embodiment of wisdom and enlightenment.

Z

Zeal

Dreams about zeal often symbolize enthusiasm, passion, or the pursuit of goals. Feeling zealous in a dream might reflect excitement or a strong drive towards achieving your objectives. Psychologically, it represents the focus on motivation and passion. Spiritually, it may signify divine encouragement or the alignment of your goals with spiritual purpose.

Zebra

A zebra in a dream often symbolizes balance, uniqueness, or duality. **Seeing a zebra** might suggest the need to embrace one's uniqueness or to balance opposing forces within oneself, while **riding a zebra** could indicate navigating life's contrasts or complexities. Psychologically, zebras can represent black-and-white thinking or the integration of opposites. Spiritually, they may signify the blending of spiritual and material worlds or the harmony of diversity.

Zip

Zippers in dreams often symbolize connection, the closing or opening of situations, or the desire for unity. **Zipping something up** might suggest the desire to close off a situation or to bring things together, while **unzipping something** could indicate the need to open up or to reveal something hidden. Psychologically, zippers can represent the mind's focus on closure, the connection between different aspects of life, or the process of revealing or concealing emotions. Spiritually, they might signify the opening of spiritual pathways, the connection between the physical and spiritual, or the closure of a cycle.

Zoning Out

Dreams about zoning out often symbolize avoidance, distraction, or the need to escape from reality. Zoning out during a significant event might reflect a desire to escape or avoid certain situations. Psychologically, it represents the focus on avoidance or distraction. Spiritually, it may signify the need for divine guidance in facing reality or addressing underlying issues.

Zoo

Zoos in dreams often symbolize containment, observation, or the exploration of different aspects of oneself. **Walking through a zoo** might suggest the desire to observe different aspects of your personality or to explore your instincts, **while seeing caged animals** could indicate feelings of confinement or the need to free yourself from restrictions. Psychologically, zoos can represent the mind's focus on self-exploration, the observation of instincts, or the containment of different aspects of the self. Spiritually, they might signify the exploration of the inner wilderness, the observation of the soul's instincts, or the desire for liberation.

Britannia: The Wall
By Richard Denham & M. J. Trow

THE END OF ROMAN BRITAIN BEGINS.

The story opens in 367 AD. Four soldiers - Justinus, Paternus, Leocadius and Vitalis - are out hunting for food supplies at an outpost of Hadrian's Wall, when the Wall comes under attack.

The four find their fort destroyed, their comrades killed, and Paternus is unable to find his wife and son. As they run south to Eboracum, they realize that this is no ordinary border raid. Ranged against the Romans at the edge of the world are four different peoples, and they have banded together under a mysterious leader who wears a silver mask and uses the name Valentinus - man of Valentia, the turbulent area north of the Wall.

Faced with questions they are hard-pressed to answer, Leocadius blurts out a story that makes the men Heroes of the Wall. Their lives change not only when Valentinus begins his lethal sweep across Britannia but as soon as Leo's lie is out in the world, growing and changing as it goes.

Goblin Market
By Maryanne Coleman

Have you ever wondered what happened to the faeries you used to believe in? They lived at the bottom of the garden and left rings in the grass and sparkling glamour in the air to remind you where they were. But that was then – now you might find them in places you might not think to look. They might be stacking shelves, delivering milk or weighing babies at the clinic. Open your eyes and keep your wits about you and you might see them.

But no one is looking any more and that is hard for a Faerie Queen to bear and Titania has had enough. When Titania stamps her foot, everyone in Faerieland jumps; publicity is what they need. Television, magazines. But that sort of thing is much more the remit of the bad boys of the Unseelie Court, the ones who weave a new kind of magic; the World Wide Web. Here is Puck re-learning how to fly; Leanne the agent who really is a vampire; Oberon's Boys playing cards behind the wainscoting; Black Annis, the bag-lady from Hainault, all gathered in a Restoration comedy that is strictly twenty-first century.

Fade
By Bethan White

There is nothing extraordinary about Chris Rowan. Each day he wakes to the same faces, has the same breakfast, the same commute, the same sort of homes he tries to rent out to unsuspecting tenants.

There is nothing extraordinary about Chris Rowan. That is apart from the black dog that haunts his nightmares and an unexpected encounter with a long forgotten demon from his past. A nudge that will send Chris on his own downward spiral, from which there may be no escape.

There is nothing extraordinary about Chris Rowan...

www.ingramcontent.com/pod-product-compliance
Lightning Source LLC
Chambersburg PA
CBHW031411150726
47989CB00002B/606